CUMBRIA
COASTAL WAY
A WALKER'S GUIDE

IAN AND KRYSIA BRODIE

Ellenbank
Press

ACKNOWLEDGEMENTS

For all their help in the creation of this walk, we would like to thank the local authorities along the route, Cumbria County Council (in particular John Studholme, John Lightfoot and Ray Singleton), English Nature, the Countryside Commission, the British Trust for Conservation Volunteers, the West Cumbria Trust, Albright & Wilson (especially their former public relations officer Mike Clay), and the host of individuals and landowners along the Way whose interest, advice and co-operation have made the route possible.

Published by Ellenbank Press, The Lathes,
Selby Terrace, Maryport, Cumbria CA15 6LX

First published 1994

Designed by Linda Blakemore

Typeset in 10/11pt Times by Deltatype Ltd,
Ellesmere Port, Cheshire
Printed and bound by St Edmundsbury Press,
Bury St Edmunds, Suffolk

British Library Cataloguing in Publication Data
A catalogue record for this book is available from
the British Library

ISBN 1 873551 10 X

CONTENTS

INTRODUCTION

On any coastline there is a constant dynamic interplay between land and sea, between destruction and creation, between erosion and deposition, and between the conflicting demands of man and nature. Nowhere is this more true than on the Cumbrian coast. From Morecambe Bay, via St Bees Head, to the Solway shore, this coastline has been shaped by thousands of years of interaction between man and nature.

Edwin Waugh, writing in 1861 in *Seaside, Lakes and Mountains of Cumbria,* said:

> Of all the English lake scenery no part lies less known than that which skirts the sea, from the ruins of Peel in Furness to Whitehaven in Cumberland: and there is none which less deserves neglect. Shut out on the east by England's wildest mountains and on the west by the Irish Channel . . . this tract of country possesses interesting relics of every race which has left a name in our history.

His comments remain true today – it is still a deeply historical coastline of fascinating extremes.

The creation of long-distance routes has been fashionable since 1935 when Tom Stephenson dreamed up the Pennine Way. Since then many hundreds of miles have received official designation or have been unofficially publicised in books or pamphlets.

Although this route is over 240 km (150 miles) long it has not been created with the long-distance walking fanatic in mind. On the contrary, the route is accessible to people of all interests and all walking abilities and is primarily designed to encourage enjoyment and understanding of the coastal land-scape. The route is well waymarked for most of its length and, because it poses few navigational problems, should appeal to walkers of all levels of experience and confidence. The route rarely climbs to an altitude of 100 m (300 ft) above sea level and can almost all be walked in short stages, particularly as public transport frequently provides an easy return to one's starting point.

The route is thus aimed at the young, the old, ramblers and amblers, families, groups, loners, photographers, geologists, geographers, industrial archaeologists, historians, naturalists, conservationists, and anyone who simply enjoys scenery. It will appeal both to visitors and local people.

This guide will serve cyclists on the Cumbria Cycle Way and tourists travelling by car or rail just as well as those on foot. Indeed the train journey from Arnside to Maryport is one of the most spectacular in the country; more so when the waves are crashing against the embankment or on clear days when there are superb views to Scotland and the Isle of Man.

FLORA AND FAUNA

There are several different types of natural habitat to be found along the coast and each supports different types of plant and animals. The coast's wildlife reveals itself to varying degrees according to the season, the state of the tides and how inconspicuous you make yourself in the landscape.

In terms of conservation, the coastal path is like a string of pearls. The pearls are the multitude of wildlife sites, many of which are designated by English Nature as National Nature Reserves (NNRs) or as Sites of Special Scientific Interest (SSSIs). In addition there are nature reserves run by bodies such as the Royal Society for the Protection of Birds (RSPB). The Cumbria Wildlife Trust and some local authorities also have an interest in reserves along the coast.

If you are remotely interested in natural history then a pair of binoculars is a must. Pocket guides to the identification of birds and flowers will also add a great deal to your appreciation.

Man has, of course, exploited the rich natural resources of the Cumbrian coast for centuries. In the estuaries people fish with nets for flounder, plaice and skate, as well as for salmon and trout. Fixed nets in the Duddon contrast with the haaf nets of the Solway or the shrimpers of Morecambe Bay. As well as fish and shrimps, there are extensive cockle and mussel beds which attract local and commercial interest. At various times in history birds' eggs have been taken for food, as at

5

Drigg, and fresh-water bivalves in the River Irt have yielded pearls.

LITERARY AND HISTORICAL CONNECTIONS

A vast quantity of prose, poetry, novels and touristic out-pourings have been written in praise of Cumbrian dales and fells. By comparison, the coastal strip has been left relatively unsung. There are, however, some exceptions to this and we have mentioned a number of books in the text which make useful and interesting background reading. Dickens and Coleridge are among the eminent literary figures who visited the area in the nineteenth century. More recently, Norman Nicholson captured the spirit of the Cumbrian coast in numerous poems.

The county of Cumbria is also of great historical interest. The coastal fringes were important places for the first settlers and many prehistoric peoples have left their mark along this route. Mesolithic hunters and gatherers may have resided here before the last ice age and immediately after it. Much later, the Romans and the Vikings played their part in shaping the landscape.

ESTUARIES

John Hartley senior of Sinkfall drowned in attempting to cross the Duddon Sands on foot. He only left home about noon and was brought back the same evening a corpse.
William Fisher, a Barrow farmer, February 1844

A major feature of interest along the walk are the beautiful wild estuaries that indent the coast of Cumbria. If you have walked the Lancashire Coastal Way or the Cistercian Way then you will have been delighted by the estuaries of the Ribble, Wyre and Lune or the Keer, Kent and Leven of Morecambe Bay. Indeed this walk begins where the Lanca-shire Coastal Way ends – on the shore of Morecambe Bay.

The Cumbria Coastal Way circumnavigates the estuaries of the Kent, Leven and Duddon, and passes the triple estuary of the Esk, Mite and Irt at Ravenglass, before rounding

Moricambe Bay and going on to the magnificent Solway. Each one of these estuaries is a scenic bonus for the coastal walker and each one is rich in history and wildlife. Indeed for some walkers they will be the highlights of the Coastal Way. Most of the estuaries are at least designated as Sites of Special Scientific Interest (SSSIs) and some qualify for designation on a worldwide scale of importance.

Sandy and muddy shores are features of the estuaries. Lugworms, sand eels, shrimps and a few bivalves burrow into the sand or mud to escape desiccation at low water. Glasswort is one of the few plants which grow in these areas. The major attractions are the feeding waders at low tide – you will see curlews, oystercatchers and shelduck, as well as sandpipers and redshank. Barren as most estuaries appear, they are biologically the most productive of habitats.

On the Ordnance Survey maps many public rights of way, both roads and bridleways, are shown on the estuaries. They are a historic feature of the sands and they were the major lines of communications in the days before turnpikes and railways. These were the trods of ancient peoples, of the Romans, and of nineteenth-century labourers seeking work in the developing industries of West Cumberland. They were the roads taken by the first Lakeland tourists and – as the graveyards of churches around the shores bear witness – they were, and still can be, the deathbeds of travellers.

We have explored the sands, shared the delights of crossing with others, and spent many hours on them photographing the light of the setting sun, listening to the calls of shelduck and oystercatchers, or simply escaping from the pressures of day-to-day life.

However, because of the dangers, no local authority who has been party to the creation of the Coastal Way will countenance an official route over the sands. There are no guides available, except for Morecambe Bay's Kent and Leven crossings. If you decide to follow these ancient routes you do so *at your own risk*. However, in the case of the Kent and Leven, we have included some notes about the guided estuary crossings in the relevant chapters of this book.

If you do wish to cross any of these estuarine sands you should avoid the winter months, and know the local tide times (often later than those quoted for the nearby ports). Most local newspapers include tide times and they are sometimes posted en route. You must also wait to cross the river channels until at least 5½ hours after the flood and be off the sands 3 hours before the next tide is due. Planning your route to arrive at these tide times is therefore exceedingly problematic. It's also worth taking a stick, to probe the unseen and unknown.

In the text, there are notes to say that under certain tides some parts of the route are either in danger of being inundated or are best walked on the sandy beach below the high water mark. These stretches include (some only at extremely high tides) the coast along from Bardsea to Rampside, around Sandscale Haws and continuing along the Duddon marshes, Haverigg to Annaside and along to Eskmeals, around Hall Waberthwaite and the Ravenglass estuaries, Drigg to Silecroft, Sellafield to St Bees, between Maryport and Silloth and also along the Solway marshes and Eden side paths. However, other shoreline stretches should be avoided at tides over 9m (29½ft).

ROUTE DIRECTIONS

Throughout the text we have used vertical rules in the left-hand margin to indicate actual route directions, as opposed to general information.

USING THIS GUIDE

The Coastal Way naturally divides into five main sections, starting with Morecambe Bay in the south and ending with the Solway Coast in the north.

Section One: Morecambe Bay
This is a gem of the north-west coastline in terms of history, natural history and scenery, with superb backdrops of the Lakeland fells and Lancashire Pennines. The bay is ringed by wildlife sites of national significance, linked with excellent limestone scenery and beautiful houses and gardens such as Levens Hall and Holker Hall. In this section Chapters 1, 2 and 3 are based on what is still an interim route.

Section Two: The Duddon Estuary
The route encircles one of Britain's most magnificent estuaries, and passes through the Lakeland town of Broughton-in-Furness and through Millom, the birthplace and lifelong home of the poet Norman Nicholson. The estuary is overshadowed by the majestic hump of Black Combe and offers a fine open prospect to the Coniston fells and to England's highest peaks, the Scafells.

Section Three: The Lake District Coast
This stretch of unspoilt countryside from Silecroft to Seascale forms the south-west fringe of the Lake District National Park and is noted for its wildlife. Inland lie spectacular dales and fells whose waters pour down to the estuary at Ravenglass where the Romans once settled and from where the miniature railway steams its way inland. Muncaster Castle and its owl-breeding sanctuary lie adjacent to the walk.

Section Four: The West Cumbrian Coast
From Seascale in the south to Maryport in the north, this is a stretch of coastline whose history was shaped by the industrial revolution. The towns of Whitehaven, Workington and

Maryport contain some superb architecture and between them lie notable natural sites like St Bees and its famous headlands. All along the route there is evidence of the interaction between man and the environment, nowhere more strikingly than at Sellafield, where BNFL's huge site lies between the sea and the fells.

Section Five: The Solway and Hadrian's Wall
This remote and seldom-visited part of the coast, between Maryport and the Scottish border, is full of historical and wildlife interest. Eventually this section will link up with the Hadrian's Wall footpath. The historic city of Carlisle is visited, before a further stretch of the Eden and Solway take us towards the Scottish border.

PLEASE NOTE
Some sections of the Way are on permissive routes and dogs *must* be kept on leads. There can be no exceptions, otherwise we will lose permission for future use. Please also keep dogs on leads in any areas where there are farm stock or wildlife – a dog off a lead can easily cause disturbance to wildlife you cannot see. If the tide is in, avoid areas where birds are roosting. During nesting times please avoid possible nesting sites, especially gravel banks above high tide level and sand dunes. Keeping to paths at these times is essential.

In general, please help to conserve the Way for future visitors and local residents. Remember the obvious – like closing gates and not dropping litter.

Readers are reminded that the publishers cannot take responsibility for accident or injury sustained on the walk. Care should always be taken to check weather conditions before setting out. In particular, you should note the information on estuaries (pp. 6–8). Suitable clothing and footwear are, of course, essential.

Every effort has been made to ensure that the information presented in this book is accurate and up to date. However if you find any changes that you feel should be included in the next edition the publishers will be pleased to hear from you.

SCOTLAND

Gretna •

Bowness •

Burgh

Carlisle

• Kirkbride

● Silloth

• Allonby

● Maryport

● Workington

● Whitehaven

CUMBRIA

• St Bees

• Seascale

• Ravenglass

Broughton

Greenodd

● Millom

Grange

• Arnside

Ulverston
Barrow

LANCS

● Morecambe

11

MAPS

In addition to the descriptions given in the text, we have provided detailed maps for the more complicated parts of the walk.

The whole of the Way can be navigated using this guide book alone, but walkers are also strongly advised to carry the relevant Ordnance Survey sheets.

Thirteen Pathfinder (1:25000) maps are required for the full route or four Landranger (1:50000) maps. The Ordnance Survey also sell a *Historical Map and Guide to Hadrian's Wall.*

Landranger Map Series
Sheet 85 Carlisle and the Solway Firth
Sheet 89 West Cumbria
Sheet 96 Barrow-in-Furness and South Lakeland
Sheet 97 Kendal and Morecambe

Pathfinder Map Series
544 (formerly NY26/36) Gretna and Eastriggs
556 (formerly NY05/15) Silloth
557 (formerly NY25/35) Carlisle (West) and Kirkbride
566 (formerly NY04/14) Aspatria
575 (formerly NY03/13) Cockermouth and Maryport
583 (formerly NX92/NY02) Workington
593 (formerly NX90/91) Whitehaven and St Bees
614 (formerly SD09/19) Ravenglass (also covered by Lake District SW area)
625 (formerly SD08/18) Broughton-in-Furness
626 (formerly SD28/38) Broughton-in-Furness and Newby Bridge
627 (formerly SD48/58) Milnthorpe
635 (formerly SD17/27) Barrow-in-Furness (North)
636 (formerly SD37/47) Grange-over-Sands
647 (formerly SD16/26) Barrow-in-Furness (South)

SECTION ONE
MORECAMBE BAY

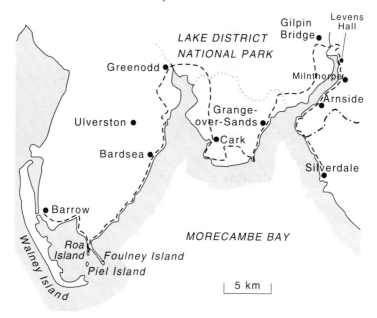

This first section of the walk takes you round a very imposing estuary where the Rivers Kent and Leven and their tributaries merge. Before tracks were turnpiked or the railways constructed, anyone travelling north had to cross the sands of Morecambe Bay. Nowadays a handful of fishermen eke out a living on the estuary in a traditional way and both rivers still possess a salaried sand pilot to guide people at low water.

Three hundred and fifty million years ago the eroded hills that once formed a central dome of rocks in primeval Lakeland gradually sank beneath the sea and were covered with marine sediments known as Carboniferous Limestone. The rock is best seen on the shores of the bay, along with Dunnerholme and Hodbarrow by the Duddon. Limestone produces a distinctive landscape and flora, and played an important part in the former iron industry of the Cumbrian coast.

14

After The Wash, Morecambe Bay is the largest area of intertidal estuarine flats in Britain. This SSSI stretches from Heysham to Walney Lighthouse and is of international significance for wintering wading birds as well as being of national significance for wintering wildfowl. Like other estuaries on the route, it provides a vital link in the chain of feeding and roosting grounds used by migrating birds. The salt marshes that fringe the bay are important for their diverse vegetation which supports a number of rare plants as well as nationally scarce invertebrates.

Most of the intertidal flats consist of fine sand and silt, with occasional muddy areas. Mussel beds are a feature of the bay, as are scars or skeers (stony outcrops which are the remains of glacial drumlins).

Wintering birds include oystercatchers, dunlin, knot, curlew, redshank, turnstone, bar-tailed godwit, grey plover and ringed plover. Some of these also nest around the bay, as do lapwing, snipe, wheatear, reed bunting, common tern, sedge warbler and linnet. Ducks include shelduck, pintail, eider, goldeneye and red-breasted merganser. Part of the bay is an RSPB reserve.

This section of the Cumbria Coastal Way is well served by the Furness Line of British Rail and by regular bus services. There is a choice of accommodation, though the only youth hostel directly on the route is at Arnside (that at Carlisle being up for sale). From Grange to Barrow the route runs parallel to, and sometimes joins, the established Cistercian Way walk.

The walker with Ordnance Survey maps could choose a variety of routes from the start to Arnside.

CHAPTER 1

SILVERDALE AND ARNSIDE TO GRANGE-OVER-SANDS

The walk starts on the border between Cumbria and Lancashire. However, for convenience, we actually start at Silverdale railway station rather than an imaginary point on the road. **Way Map 1** includes the route from the county boundary at Silverdale to Arnside. Details of the Silverdale area will be found in the forthcoming guide book to the Lancashire Coastal Way.

Key to Way Maps

– – – – –	route		■	buildings
═══════	road		g	gate
::::::::::	track		kg	kissing gate
··········	path		s	stile
──────────	railway		lc	level crossing
·–·–·–·	county boundary		St	station
············	National Park boundary		b	bridge
•–•–•–•	field boundary		fb	footbridge
◠◠	shoreline		PH	public house
			CP	car park
～～	stream		PC	public convenience
～～	river		🌳	wood (deciduous)
⬭	pond/tarn		🌲	wood (coniferous)
//₁₁\\	steep slope			

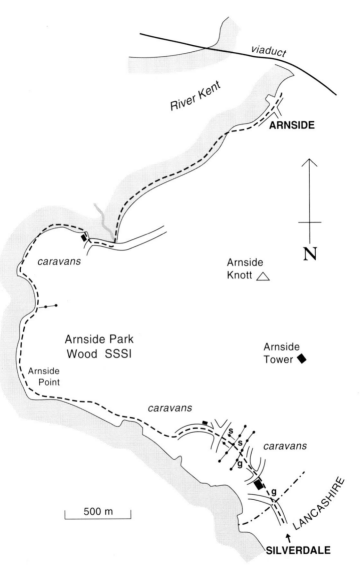

viaduct

River Kent

ARNSIDE

N

caravans

Arnside
Knott △

Arnside Park
Wood SSSI

Arnside
Tower ◆

Arnside
Point

caravans

s

s

g

caravans

g

LANCASHIRE

500 m

SILVERDALE

Way Map 1: Start to Arnside

This section of the walk traverses Arnside Point's scenic small cliffs and the rich woodlands between the coast and Arnside Knott. Just inland from the first caravan site lies Arnside Tower – an imposing pele tower built in the fifteenth century to provide safety from Scottish raiders. Details of the building are to be found in *Archaeological Sites of the Lake District* by Tom Clare (see Bibliography).

The bulk of Arnside Knott forms a distinctive feature of this first stretch of the walk. It is also an SSSI and the designated area stretches from the shore to the far side of the lumpy fell. As we progress beyond the second caravan site to the shoreside area, we enter herb-rich calcareous grasslands and woods which are home to several butterfly species. The Scotch argus, the Duke of Burgundy fritillary, high brown fritillary, pearl-bordered fritillary, northern brown argus, grayling and green hairstreak have all been sighted.

Common lizards flit across the stones or bathe in the sun, whilst the trees include Lancastrian whitebeam, small-leaved lime, an uncommon whitebeam and the wild service tree.

The start of the walk, in the Silverdale–Arnside area, has associations with Charlotte and Emily Brontë, who stayed here when there was an outbreak of fever in Haworth. There is also a connection with Elizabeth Gaskell, Charlotte's biographer, who frequently stayed in the area and loved to watch the sun set over the Kent estuary from Gibraltar Tower where she wrote parts of most of her books.

SILVERDALE TO THE START

Leave the station, turn right along the road and cross to the stile next to the gate. Enter the golf course and climb the slight rise ahead, cut across the fairway and pick up a track which leads right and up to a small kissing gate. The path over the course is waymarked.

Turn right on the road and take the enclosed path between the garage and bungalow (No. 6 Bankwell) on the left. This path goes straight through some woodland and descends to a stile. Use the path directly across Lambert's Meadow and cross the footbridge but not the stile ahead.

Go left, following the wall, and cross the stile in the corner of the field. Follow the right-hand wall and continue as it bends right. Then continue on the track, past some houses. When you reach the road, turn left.

At Silverdale Green, take the first road to the right and follow it until it joins the main road. Turn right, and go along into Silverdale village.

Go straight ahead at the first road junction in the village (the road to the right leads to the shops) and follow the road round to the left. After the cottage on the right is a gate and then a wall. (At low tide you can continue to the end of the road and turn right along the foreshore, to reach the cove with the cave.) At the end of this wall a ramp leads up, by a footpath sign, to a stile where you enter a field. Cross the middle of the long field and go over another stile, then walk to the far right-hand corner of the field above the small knolls. Beyond another stile an enclosed path leads down to the foreshore where you will find a cove with a small cave in the cliff.

Go through the gate on your right and follow the road up, away from the shore, to a road junction. Turn left, and after a few hundred metres you will be on the county boundary.

COUNTY BOUNDARY TO ARNSIDE

Leave the road through a gate on your right and go past the right-hand side of the caravan site buildings. Cross the site access road, then go down Oak Drive access road which is facing you.

After about 100m (110 yds) follow the path down left off the road and through a clump of trees. Go through the gate in the fence and then over a stile which takes you over the wall ahead. Follow the left-hand wall along, go through the gap at the end and then over a stile to reach the road. Cross the road and follow a metalled track, on entering the caravan site, called Park Point Drive (signed to Far Arnside). Go through the caravan site and continue into the woods on the far side, after bearing left opposite Knott Drive.

Once in the wood you reach a junction. Turn left and the

path soon begins to follow the small cliffs overlooking the Kent Estuary and Grange-over-Sands. The path is distinct and narrow in places.

Squirrels and lizards as well as birds of the estuary can be seen. Arnside Point, St Bees Heads, Humphrey Head, Dunnerholme and just south of Annaside Banks provide the main rocky shore features along the route. Animals such as limpets, barnacles, winkles and mussels can be found on the rocks and in the pools near Annaside.

The cliffside path continues until it meets a ruined wall by a footpath sign. Turn left through the gap in the wall by the four-trunked oak tree (signed to White Creek Bay) and follow the path through more woodland. You are now just inside the shoreline but out of view of the bay. Keep to the left of the caravans and eventually, on meeting a broader track from the right, go left on to the shingle of the bay.

Approaching Arnside Point along the Kent Estuary, Morecambe Bay.

Turn right along the edge of the bay until, at the end of the shingle, sloping rock leads you up to the clifftop. Turn left on to this path, ignore any paths leading down to the shore, and continue through a wood until – just short of a field – the right-hand fence forces you down on to the shore. Turn right on the shore, pass the farmhouse and continue along the track until it becomes a metalled road. Go left (to leave the road) here and follow the shore round the bluff and eventually to the promenade in Arnside. Continue round the seafront to the railway station.

Until the coming of the railway Arnside was a quiet village with a pleasant old inn, the Fighting Cocks, dating back to 1660. It was originally a fishing village with a small salt-making industry and later became the only port in the old county of Westmorland. The promenade was constructed in 1897 when the railways brought an influx of tourists to the village.

The railway company built the pier at Arnside for ships, because their viaduct had obstructed the passage of ships to the port of Milnthorpe. The village had a famous boat-building company, Crossfields, which made trawlers to operate in Morecambe Bay. These sleek boats were designed like yachts and, until the advent of the marine diesel engine, carried an enormous amount of sail.

The tides at Arnside are very strong and many people come to the estuary side to watch the tidal bore race towards the viaduct. The coastal walker will find most requirements catered for in the shops opposite the promenade. Arnside also has one of the few youth hostels on the route.

ARNSIDE TO GRANGE
If you do not wish to follow the route round the magnificent Kent estuary, you will miss some superb estuary scenery, the delights of Levens Hall and some varied wildlife. These advantages more than compensate for the bits of road walking involved. However if you prefer to go directly from Arnside to Grange-over-Sands there are two possibilities.

21

Alternative 1: Crossing the Sands

The current Queen's Guide to the Kent Sands is Cedric Robinson (see Useful Addresses). Notwithstanding this historic title, the monasteries were actually the first to employ guides, or carters, to ensure that people passed safely across the sands.

On some days Cedric leads walks from Arnside across to Grange but you will need to contact him, on Grange-over-Sands (05395) 32165, to find out if you can join such a group. Midweek crossings are unlikely. Cedric is also a fisherman and an author of several books on Morecambe Bay.

Alternative 2: The Railway

Under no circumstances are you allowed to walk over the viaduct. Trains run from Arnside to Grange if you must take a short cut, though this is really too easy an alternative.

The viaduct has 50 piers and when it was being built it was found that borings would have to go down nearly 30 m (98 ft) to reach suitable foundations. The problem was solved by sinking hollow iron piles nearly 10 m (33 ft) long, with a broad iron disc as a foot, to act as pier supports. The first train crossed in 1857 and it spelt the end not only of the cross-sands route but also of ships going up to Sandside and Milnthorpe – this despite the broader arch in the viaduct made to allow for this problem. The embankments constructed by the railway company enabled about 400 hectares (1000 acres) of land to be claimed from the estuary.

ARNSIDE TO LEVENS BRIDGE

The walk route continues along Arnside Promenade as far as the railway station. Go up to the platform, cross the footbridge and then turn right, through a gap in the fence, beyond the glass shelter. Go down to the bed of the former railway and follow it right. Where the track splits, go through the left-hand gate.

The old track bed is now a sea defence wall which takes us to Sandside. As you walk along, there are superb views of the Kent estuary. And the Lakeland peaks peep over the foothills: firstly the Coniston Fells and the Fairfield Horse-shoe; then the Kentmere fells; and later the Langdales and the Howgills.

When a filled-in road bridge blocks the way, go down to your left. Walk along the foreshore to reach the road, and follow it through Sandside until you reach the Ship Inn. Beyond the pub car park, turn right on to an enclosed path to reach a metalled track. Go left along this, ignoring any paths to the right. You will pass below the massive limestone quarry and eventually re-emerge on to the road.

Go straight across the road and down the steps by the footpath sign. The path skirts the estuary and, after a stile, uses the old railway bed again. To your left, the River Bela meanders out to reach the more distant River Kent.

When the stony track bed gives way to grass, look for a path that slopes down the embankment to the left. Then, round the point, follow the banks of the Bela along the right-hand fence until the fence meets the river bank. Use the kissing gate to enter the field on your right. Follow the bankside fence, pass the weir, and go towards the superb single-arched bridge. The kissing gate to the road lies to the right of the bridge.

Milnthorpe, just beyond the bridge, is quite a busy village, with a variety of shops. Dallam Tower, which lies just over the road from the kissing gate, was built in 1720, and fallow deer roam the parkland.

Go over the bridge, turn left and take the first road off to your left. Continue down the minor road which roughly follows the now narrowing Kent estuary. Local people go through the stile next to the first gate on the left, through the wood and follow the embankment top, parallel to the road. When the embankment veers away from the road, go over the stile to rejoin the road. When the road bends right, turn right, then first left, and right again at College Green Farm. This takes you up to the A6 which you follow to the left to reach Levens Hall and Bridge over the River Kent.

Levens Hall

The Elizabethan Levens Hall, with its superb topiary gardens, is worth setting aside a couple of hours to visit as you pass by. The famous house, occupied by its owners, the Bagots, has a great deal of interest to attract all members of the family.

The house is open from Sunday to Thursday from Easter until the end of September and admission tickets can be bought to the house and gardens or just the gardens between 11 am and 4.30 pm.

The gardens are famous for their topiary – the hedges were planted around 1700 – and the head gardener is only the tenth to hold that position since 1692. The fantastically shaped topiary work interspersed with colourful bedding plants, the ancient beech hedge, the seventeenth-century garden and the herb garden are only a few of its delights. There is even a children's adventure playground amongst the greenery.

The house was originally built as a pele tower, to keep the de Redman family safe from marauding Scots in 1250–1300. Their cousins, the Bellinghams, turned the fortress into a gentleman's residence towards the end of the sixteenth century, and a wing and brewhouse were later added.

Inside, the house still has a wonderfully lived-in air; the notice on the front door tells you not to ring the bell, just come in. The oak-panelled walls add warmth to the building and every nook and cranny has something interesting on display. Most items are well labelled and there are helpful staff members on hand. The house comprises several bedrooms, a dining room, a library, a couple of drawing rooms and, when you enter through the front door, the Great Hall.

The original sixteenth-century decor, including the plastered ceilings, wood-panelled walls and painted leather wall coverings, fit well with the furniture and works of art of many periods, and with the comfortable carpets and furniture used daily by the Bagot family.

Outside you will find a shop, a pleasant café, and a collection of model steam engines. On Sundays and Bank Holiday Mondays, when it's fine, a showman's locomotive and a 1901 steam car may be seen in motion.

Levens Hall.

Across the A6 from the Hall is the beautiful Levens Hall park. Here are black fallow deer from Norway, and rare Bagot goats. Down the river you might see a heron, dippers and even mergansers.

LEVENS BRIDGE TO GRANGE

Cross the bridge, turn left along the A590 and take a path into the wood by the site of the old ford over the Kent. This saves a little road walking and takes you along the river bank on its last stretch before it becomes part of the estuary. (The wood is noticeably aromatic at ransom flowering time.) You re-emerge on the A590 by a junction. Go left and take the first left-hand turning down the narrow road to Low Levens Farm (signed to Sampool Caravan Park).

Low Levens, or Nether Levens, probably dates from the early sixteenth century. The house has some superb elliptical chimney stacks, though the south cross wing is in ruins. On the east side, part of the building, with mullioned and transomed windows, was added in 1594.

Continue to just beyond High Sampool Farm and, after the overhead wires, turn right down the enclosed track which becomes a bridleway (to Sampool Bridge). Continue round the right-hand bend and rejoin the A590.

Go left and cross the River Gilpin where the walk first passes into the Lake District National Park. Once over the bridge, take the first turn left and go down the tarmac farm access road to reach, after 1.6 km (1 mile), High Foulshaw Farm.

Continue on the road as it turns right and then left. Go through the gate on the left, follow the left-hand boundary and, after the next gate, turn right. Follow the foot of the embankment and, after it veers off to the left, continue along the enclosed lane. When the embankment comes back to your track, pass through the gate to your right, and follow the embankment along until you come to the first rocky outcrop and gated track at Birkswood Point.

Follow the track over the next small section of embankment and then continue through the gate to Cat Cottage. Pass Cat Cottage, and its access track off to the right, and go straight ahead to the edge of Crag Wood, a Woodland Trust site. Almost opposite the gate into the wood, turn right and cross the footbridge with stiles at either end. In the field on the other side, pass the end of a hedge and then cross a stile adjacent to an overhead wire pole. Where the next hedge becomes a fence, go straight on along the old embankment to cross a further stile with a gate and a section of wall to the left, cross to the far left-hand corner of the field ahead, go over a stile, then cross to the far left-hand corner of the next field and go over a further stile, to reach a road.

Turn left along the road, right at the first junction and pass through Meathop, a small hamlet of stone-built houses and farms where the road often looks like part of a farmyard. Keep left at the two road junctions, pass further houses and ignore the entrances to Woodlands and the former hospital at Meathop.

Meathop Woods and Quarry

Meathop woods and quarry, another SSSI, are found on the limestone hillock by the railway line, and this hillock has forced the route inland around its northern slopes. The native deciduous woodland on the hillock is relatively undisturbed and has served as an outdoor laboratory for many years. Along with a range of trees there is an interesting population of plants and invertebrates. The quarry displays strata laid down 335 million years ago which are rich in fossils yielding clues about the carboniferous environment.

The road now descends via Low Meathop Farm, crosses the River Winster and continues by the railway into Grange-over-Sands.

On the right, downstream on the River Winster, can be seen Castle Head. This field study centre was once the house of local ironmaster John Wilkinson, who is credited with building the first iron boat. It is said that his coffin, made of iron, was temporarily lost in the sands of the Kent whilst being brought to his house.

Grange-over-Sands

In his book *Cumbria*, John Parker describes Grange-over-Sands as 'a grey limestone town of prosperous-looking houses overlooking Morecambe Bay'. He says 'it was the railway and the area's mild mean temperatures which caused its expansion as a tourist resort and attracted builders of middle-class houses. The vast sands of the bay are rather muddy, and this probably saved Grange from rivalling Blackpool.' With its hillside location, its famous duck pond and attractive promenade complete with palm trees, the town is very popular with retired people.

A view of the Kent Estuary from above Grange-over-Sands, with Arnside Knott and snowcapped Ingleborough beyond.

CHAPTER 2

GRANGE-OVER-SANDS
TO ULVERSTON

GRANGE TO HUMPHREY HEAD

From Grange railway station use the bridge to go under the railway line and follow the promenade. Pass the former open air swimming pool and, at the end of the promenade, go back under the railway. Continue along the path or road nearest the railway, eventually going down Cart Lane and passing Guides Farm to reach some steps up to the road. Turn left down the road to Kent's Bank station and toilets.

At high tide, climb the steep road opposite the station and turn left at the junction at the top of the hill. The narrower road now goes down towards Allithwaite village. If you continue straight ahead you will come to the main part of the village and a pub (which serves good food) called Guide over the Sands. See **Way Map 2** for details of the high tide route from the nearby Pheasant Inn to Humphrey Head.

To take the low tide route from Kent's Bank station, cross the level crossing, turn right, follow the railway embankment and go round Kirkhead End. Then, after, a further stretch by the railway line, you will reach the side of Wyke Farm where you meet the high tide route from Allithwaite. Continue on to pass the farm.

If you wish to take a short cut, turn right down the narrow enclosed Pigeon Cote Lane to the road on the western side of the Head. However it is worth continuing

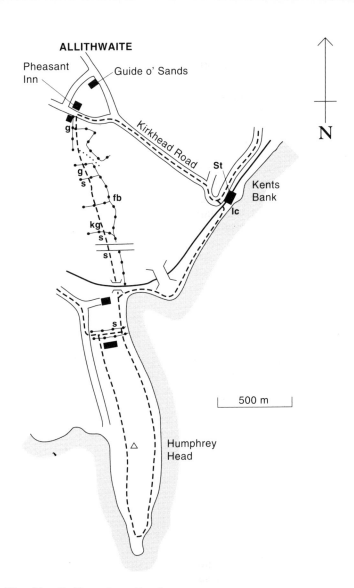

Way Map 2: Humphrey Head.

along the shoreside path which takes you through Humphrey Head Wood and on to Humphrey Head Point.

Humphrey Head SSSI

Humphrey Head is a dramatic limestone promontory with three main habitats – the west-facing cliffs, the grassland along the ridge, and the eastern-facing deciduous wood. As at Meathop, the geological exposures reveal Lower Carboniferous rocks formed 325 million years ago.

The anthills and small outcrops of limestone pavement add interest to this area where, according to local legend, the last wolf in England was slain. The spa or 'Holy Well' on the eastern side is a foul-tasting spring but a few centuries ago people visited it for its alleged curative properties.

The area is open to the public and forms the Joy Ketchen Nature Reserve managed by the Cumbria Wildlife Trust. Dogs *must* be kept on leads.

HUMPHREY HEAD TO HOLKER HALL

From Humphrey Head Point, walk along the ridge over the top of the Head and continue, with the cliffs on your left, until you come to a track leading to an outdoor pursuits centre. Go left on the track to reach the road.

Turn right on the road and then left to go parallel with the railway. Turn left again at the junction below Wraysholme Farm with its pele tower. After a long stretch of road you come to the next junction where you go left down a long straight road past an old airfield. This is a parachute centre, where you might want to pause and watch people taking the drop.

Fisherfolk catch flukes, cockles and shrimps from the sands of Morecambe Bay and they can often be seen at low tide from the Head. Once they took their nets on to the sands with horse-drawn carts but now the remaining few use carts hauled by tractors. Sandgate and West Plains, places shortly to be met on the route, are where the fishermen leave dry land for the sands of the bay.

Shrimps are usually caught between March and the first frosts. A local co-operative boils them for market and Morecambe Bay shrimps are a fine local delicacy. However catches vary from year to year. Fluke, or flounder, also disappear with the frosts.

At West Plains, where the road bends left, carry on to the saltings ahead and turn sharp right to follow the embankment to its end near Cowpren Point. Continue round the Point and follow the shoreline past Cannon Winder Farm with its superb chimneys to arrive at Sandgate. From here you have a choice of routes to Ulverston, but eventually we hope Holker Estates will permit a pleasant path adjacent to the estuary.

One direct way from Sandgate is to walk across the sands to Chapel Island and then come ashore at Canal Foot. Start by aiming for Chapel Island, then go up the estuary aiming for Coniston Old Man until you are opposite Canal Foot. Before attempting this route you *must* phone the sand pilot, on Ulverston (0229) 580935, and look back at the basic rules on estuaries (p. 8). There is a three- or four-hour period, depending on the tide, in which you can safely cross before the turning tide affects the route. This gives you sufficient time for the crossing and a short visit to Chapel Island.

Chapel Island

In his book *Furness and Cartmel* Knapp-Fisher describes Chapel Island as the 'ancient shrine and seat of a monk or priest who succoured and prayed for those in peril on the sands.' He also says the chapel was set up less than 150 years ago as:

'ancient ruins' to add beauty to natural sites as was the fashion; the wall, with lancet windows and a circular window on Chapel Island, is on the very ancient foundations of a chapel originally founded centuries ago by the monks of Conishead Priory. The island was undoubtedly a resting-place for the Furness monks when they crossed the estuaries to their fisheries.

According to Father Thomas West's *Antiquities of Furness*, the Conishead monks used to say mass for travellers on Chapel Island about a mile from Bardsea shore, but there is little evidence to support this. The present building, according to Norman Nicholson's *Greater Lakeland*, is 'a mock ruin set up by Colonel Braddyll who built the Gothic-revival Conishead Priory in the early nineteenth century' (a verdict which supports Knapp-Fisher's story).

If you choose to walk the sands route you will be in good historical company. The monks of Conishead and Furness came this way, as did John Wesley and George Fox. Early tourists and guide-book writers used the route, as did Robert Bruce's army and the troops of Lambert Simnel. So busy were the sands, and so treacherous, that the monks had to appoint official guides to both the Kent Sands and the Leven Sands.

Hindle records that the 3-mile crossing of the Leven often caused more problems than those of the longer Keer–Kent estuaries. Guides evidently advised travellers not to stop, as the sand under their carriage wheels would be washed away. The sands traffic finally disappeared when the railway line was completed in 1857.

From Sandgate, follow the road inland. After a short distance turn left down a signposted enclosed path which leads over a very high railway bridge and then descends to the Engine Inn in Cark. Beyond the inn turn left and follow the road up to Holker Hall.

Another alternative is to turn right at the Engine Inn and take the train from nearby Cark-in-Cartmel station to Ulverston. You can then walk down through the town centre and along the canal towpath to Canal Foot. Though this is hardly challenging for the walker, interesting views of the estuary can be obtained from the train.

Holker Hall
If you intend to visit Holker Hall, Gardens and Park, please note that they are open (except on Saturdays) from Easter Sunday to the last Sunday in October (10.30am–6pm).

Holker Hall, home of Lord Cavendish, with its splendid gardens.

The Hall is the former home of the Dukes of Devonshire, from whom the present owners, Lord and Lady Hugh Cavendish, are descended. As well as the house there are superb gardens, woodlands, a large deer park, the Lakeland Motor Museum, a craft and country life museum, guided discovery walks, an adventure playground, a baby animal house and, naturally, a cafeteria. In spite of all this commercialism the house and grounds retain an atmosphere of comfortable tranquillity.

Holker Hall was first built in the seventeenth century by the Preston family. It was inherited by the Lowthers and then the Cavendishes. The land originally came from Cartmel Priory when it was annexed by the Duchy of Lancaster during the Dissolution. The Bishopric of Chester then bought the land from the Duchy and sold it to the Prestons, a local family. The first house was built in 1604 but was temporarily lost when the son had his estates sequestered by Parliament because he entertained Royalist troops. He had to buy it back.

The principal rooms include the library with over 3500 volumes, some of them brought from Chatsworth in Derbyshire. There are works by the scientist Henry Cavendish and his microscope can be seen in the room. The light switches are hidden behind imitation books with humorous titles positioned beside the doorway.

The gardens – all 9 hectares (22 acres) of them – make a splendid foil to the house. A well-illustrated guide book is available, as is a guide to the woodland walks.

HOLKER TO HAVERTHWAITE
From the front of the Hall a possible route goes left along the B5278 road, then back into the National Park, and to the bridge over the River Leven at Low Wood near Haverthwaite. (The mosses next to the road are part of Roudsea Wood SSSI and National Nature Reserve.) Walking along the road is not recommended however.

Way Map 3 covers the route from near Holker to Nancy Tarn. Continue on the B5278, past the gates of Holker Hall, until you reach a cottage on the right-hand side of the

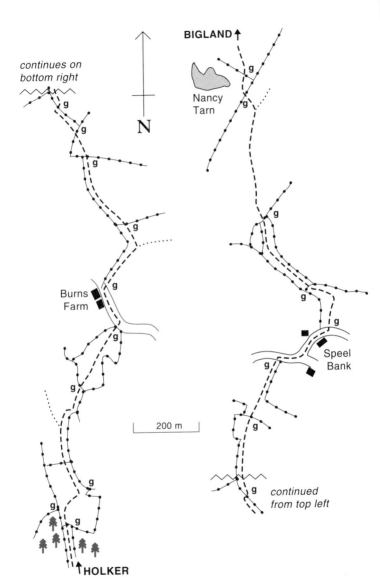

continues on
bottom right

BIGLAND

Nancy
Tarn

g

g

N

g

g

Burns
Farm

g

g

g

g

Speel
Bank

g

g

200 m

g

g

g

g

g

continued
from top left

g

g

HOLKER

Way Map 3: Holker to Bigland

road after the speed signs. Just before the cottage, go up right through the wood and through a gate to enter a field by a road. Go left along the track by the left-hand wall with a crowning thorn hedge until you come to a gate in a wall. Turn left immediately before this gate and go through another gate to follow an enclosed track.

Follow this track as it bends right, goes through woodland and re-enters the fields by a gate. Go along the left-hand wall to a further gate which gives you views of Ulverston, the Leven estuary and the railway viaduct. Do not go through this gate but turn right and follow the track up the field, parallel to the overhead wires, to arrive at a further gate.

Turn left before this gate and follow the signposted bridleway near the right-hand wall. Go through the gate in the fence and then take the right-hand fork, keeping by the wall. Go through the next gate on your right and along the obvious path that descends gently beneath the left-hand wall. Pass through a fence line and walk straight ahead to a gate in a wall, near a caravan. Go forward to the farm access track and follow it to the yard of Burns Farm.

Opposite the entrance to Burns Farm, turn right through a gate on the right of the barn and go down the left-hand boundary of the field. Turn left after the old gate posts and follow the left-hand boundary through two fields. Go through a gate in the left-hand corner of the second field, and cross another field to pass through a further gate. Follow the right-hand wall, go through the first gate way and then follow the left-hand wall. When this wall bends left, go straight ahead to pass through a further gate. Pass the overhead wires and continue straight ahead, following the right-hand wall, to go through a further gate in the field corner.

Here you will find a track. Turn right along it, bear left in Speel Bank Farm, and after a further gate the track becomes tarred. Go left through a gate and up the field below the left-hand wall. When you are a little higher, swing left to pass through a gate in the far corner of the field. A distinct track leads through a wood to a further gate and on to open fell. From here there are excellent views of the Leven estuary and the Lake District.

After the gate go straight ahead to pick up a track which you follow to the right of a perched boulder. Continue on this rutted track, and when it begins to descend towards a pylon pass through a gate in the left-hand wall. Go through the next gate in the fence, go half-left beneath a rocky outcrop and drop down to the road, via two gates, to the left of a house.

Turn right on the road and then left down the house drive, keeping to the immediate left of the house at the end of the drive. Go through a small gate into a field. Cross the field near the right-hand wall and pass through a further gate some 20 m (22 yds) below the field corner. A distinct path by the left-hand fence now takes you through a wood and, after a second gate, into a field.

Turn left in the field, and keep all walls to your left, to pass an open vista of the estuary before descending towards Bigland Tarn. After the gate turn left, away from the water. Contour left, past the footpath sign, and then drop down to the lowest part of the land ahead. Go through a small gate in the wall and continue steeply down through the woods, ignoring any tracks crossing your path, to re-emerge on the B5278 Holker Road. Turn right to reach the bridge over the Leven.

Low Wood, Haverthwaite, lies just off the road to the right. This small hamlet was formerly a gunpowder works and now has a craft studio.

HAVERTHWAITE TO ULVERSTON

Just before the bridge over the Leven, turn left down the private road and when it bends slightly left, away from the river, cross the stile on your right. Follow the riverbank path through the first field, cross the stile and then go half-left to cross a footbridge over a ditch where the hedge from the left meets the river bank. In the third field continue along the riverside path and cross a stile to rejoin the road. Turn right down the road to reach Roudsea Wood.

Roudsea Wood and Mosses National Nature Reserve

This is a composite site of exceptionally diverse and ancient woodlands lying almost at sea level. On the east the site merges with an extensive estuarine lowland raised mire system and, to the west, saltmarsh. These habitats support an outstanding variety of flowering plants and invertebrates.

Roudsea Wood itself sits on two ridges of different rocks that give rise to calcareous and acidic soils as well as to bog and fen conditions. It is these different soils which have produced the very diverse woodlands.

Besides a wide range of trees, flowers, endangered flies, nationally vulnerable beetles and other invertebrates there are more than 50 species of birds, including nightjar, woodcock, curlew, owls and the great spotted woodpecker. The adder, grass snake, slow worm and common lizard are recorded and the mammals listed include the red, roe and fallow deer, badger, red squirrel, otter, stoat, weasel, mink, mole, common and pigmy shrew, dormouse and hare. The area is also of geological interest and the caves in the limestone strata have been studied intensively. Access permits and a leaflet can be obtained from English Nature (see Useful Addresses).

Follow the road past the entrance to the nature reserve, through a wooded area and down through fields until it bends sharply left. Leave the road here and go through the gate straight ahead into a field. Follow the left-hand boundary through a gate and then walk along by the right-hand fence to cross an embankment. Go along by the left-hand fence to a stile and then cross the fine footbridge (which replaced a former railway bridge) over the River Leven. You arrive on the A590 opposite Greenodd. The main street is just across the road and there are some shops.

Turn left down the road by the fence next to the Leven

and continue until you reach a car park. From here the Way is still under development. At present (1994) you continue along the verge by the A590 and after 2km (1¼ miles) take the second narrow road off to the left. Keep left at the next junction, follow the road across former and current railway bridges, pass the impressive chimneys of Plumpton Hall and continue down to the shore of the Leven estuary.

Follow the shoreside path to a road, some toilets and Ulverston Canal Foot. Here also is the Bay Horse Hotel, renowned for its excellent food.

ULVERSTON

Ulverston Canal is one of only three canals built in Cumbria. There is the Lancaster which runs from Wigan (though in continuous water terms from Preston) to Kendal. This is only navigable in Lancashire. Then there is the short but wide Ulverston Canal which is the only one full of water but with its sea exit blocked. Finally there is the Port Carlisle Link.

The market square in Ulverston.

In the eighteenth century Ulverston was an iron ore port where up to 150 ships were based. However, with the development of Liverpool, many ships moved to gain trade. After the opening of the canal, in 1796, the nearby Newlands mining company built an ore quay and trade from coastal loading sites like Conishead Bank decreased to nothing. Unfortunately the canal suffered from the vagaries of the shifting Leven channel which could, by moving away from the west bank, make it impossible for larger ships to pass.

Nevertheless the canal made Ulverston an important sea port, until it was eclipsed by the railway in the mid-nineteenth century as well as suffering from problems caused by a silting channel. In its heyday, in 1846, 946 ships of 61,000 tons used the canal. Iron ore, pig iron, bar iron, Kirkby Moor slate, limestone and grain were shipped out and Wigan coal was shipped in.

If you wish to go into Ulverston town centre follow the towpath, from Canal Foot to Canal Head. Ulverston is an attractive market town with a good choice of Hartley's pubs. The main attractions for visitors are Hoad Hill and its landlocked lighthouse, the Laurel and Hardy Museum, and the Cumbria Crystal glass workshops. The next section of the walk, to Barrow, starts from Canal Foot.

CHAPTER 3

ULVERSTON TO BARROW-IN-FURNESS

CANAL FOOT TO CONISHEAD

From the Bay Horse Inn at Canal Foot, Ulverston, take the road inland from the shore with the massive Glaxo plant on your right. Take the first road off to the left and keep left after the Sea View Pub.

Glaxo

The Glaxochem works occupy the site of the former North Lonsdale Ironworks – hence the slag heaps on the seaward side of the last stretch of the walk. (The ironworks stopped producing iron in 1938.) The Ulverston plant is the multinational Glaxo group's largest single manufacturing unit and one of the largest antibiotic-producing plants in the world.

Since 1948, starting with penicillin, many thousands of tonnes of antibiotics have been manufactured here. Specific moulds are fermented and the antibiotics are then extracted from the fermentation broth; they are further purified before being packed in sterilised containers. The plant products include penicillin, cephalosporin, griseofulvin (for ringworm treatment) and vitamin B12 (to combat pernicious anaemia).

Follow this road, cross a dyke and then go through a gate on your left to enter a field. In the field go to your right, passing behind the grounds of the house, then follow the right-hand boundary as far as the gate to the left of the chimney.

The chimney is that of a former brickworks. When the works were demolished it had to be left to continue its other function of guiding ships to Canal Foot.

Go along the road ahead and follow it left, passing the old railway crossing house, to reach the shoreline track. Follow this down to a wall at Conishead Bank and the bottom of the grounds of Conishead Priory.

Conishead Bank
Conishead Bank is the source, according to Alfred Fell's *The Early Iron Industry of Furness and District*, of the oldest reference to one of the local industries. The relevant document is a deed from William de Lancaster III (1220–46), granting land for a forge, a mine and dead wood to burn to the Prior of Conishead.

In the eighteenth century, iron ore from nearby mines was shipped from Conishead Bank. This was also where the ancient road from Cartmel came ashore, as it was then the only place where cliffs and peat mosses did not obstruct access to the land. The track then crossed the Furness peninsula and is referred to by some as a Roman road. In fact the metalled surfaces are probably medieval, with one section over the marshy Goldmire valley forming a typical Bronze Age 'corduroy' road of logs.

Opposite the short section of wall along the estuary side is a woodland path leading up to the remarkable Conishead Priory.

Conishead Priory
The existing house on the site of Conishead Priory was built as a private residence in 1821 but later became a hydro (a branch railway linking it to Ulverston opened in 1874), then a Durham Miners Convalescent Home, and, more recently, an Institute for Buddhist studies. The Gothic Revival house was built for Colonel Braddyll, and designed by Philip Wyatt, when the cross-sands route was still the main line of communication with the booming industries of western Cumbria.

Conishead Priory, now a Buddhist centre.

The priory was originally founded by Gamel de Pennington during the twelfth century as a hospital for relief of 'the poor, decrepit, indigent and lepers', and later became an Augustinian priory. In about 1180 William de Lancaster, Baron of Kendal and Lord of the Manor of Ulverston under Furness Abbey, granted to the priory all Conishead, the church at Ulverston, and 40 acres in its fields, a salt works and the rights of turbary (cutting peat or turf), pasture, pannage (feeding pigs on fallen acorns), and timber-taking in his woods of Furness and the Manor of Ulverston – a grant which probably replaced the earlier one by Gamel de Pennington.

From time to time the priory received various gifts of land and this evidently caused friction between Conishead and Furness Abbey, often ending in legal disputes. Settlements of such disputes were frequently in favour of the larger Furness Abbey. The date at which the hospital ceased to function is uncertain. Until they surrendered to the Dissolution in the summer of 1536, the priors of Conishead had to maintain the guides over the Leven Sands. On Dissolution, the Prior was given the vicarage of Orton and the seven Canons a pension of

£1.17s.8d each. Sale of the priory goods raised a total of £333 (Cartmel only brought £275).

The current house is dominated by two towers over 30 m (98 ft) high with a traceried window below showing the principal benefactors of the original priory. After its use as a miners' convalescent home it fell into disrepair before being taken over by the Manjushri Institute as a centre for Tibetan Buddhist studies. They have largely repaired the damage suffered during the earlier period of neglect in spite of scarce financial resources. The house and grounds are a fine testament to the work done and both can be visited. A guide book is available which gives information on the house, its history, the story of its saving and restoration, its woods and grounds and about the Buddhists who now live and work in it. For up-to-date information on opening days and times telephone Ulverston 0229 584029.

The Braddylls, who had Conishead built in 1821, were originally a Lancashire family who moved to the Ulverston area from over the sands. John Braddyll had purchased Whalley Abbey from the Crown. His grandson, also called John, was commissioned to survey the Queen's woods in Furness, thus beginning the family connection with Furness.

The Victorian love affair with all things Gothic has been well documented but the Bradylls took it to its limits. Apparently one of them had a small cell built in the grounds of the house and actually paid a man to act as a hermit for the entertainment of his guests.

CONISHEAD TO ALDINGHAM

Continue along the shoreside until you come to the second road towards the shore near a small chemical works. Go up this lane but turn left behind a hillock to reach the shore again. The shoreline is part of Bardsea Country Park and you will find toilets and ice-cream vendors by the roadside.

The village atop the hill is Bardsea, with its distinctive church spire built of local limestone. There is a pub in the village and a pleasant stretch of beach.

At low tide it is possible (and much safer than following the road) to walk along the foreshore from Bardsea towards Rampside where a sea wall takes you from the sands. En route there are points of interest at Sea Wood, Baycliffe, Aldingham and Rampside.

Sea Wood SSSI, now owned by the Woodland Trust, is a rare example of a woodland on boulder clay overlying limestone. This ancient woodland site thus has a diverse composition and the flora has benefited from being left ungrazed. If you walk on the shoreline a small cliff marks the boundary of the wood which supports a variety of plants.

Aldingham has some interesting buildings and is also the site of a motte castle. Its church is dedicated to St Cuthbert and stands very close to the shore. Indeed the sea appears to have claimed part of its graveyard. The church was rebuilt in 1866 but part of the stonework is probably late twelfth century or early thirteenth century, as is the priest's doorway.

Just south of Aldingham, if you use the road, you arrive at Moat Farm to your right. Beyond the farm a path leads over an eroded drumlin which is the site of Aldingham Castle. The path rejoins the road just short of Newbiggin.

The seventeenth-century Rampside Hall farmhouse, with its ridge display of twelve chimneys, can be seen from here.

FOULNEY, ROA AND PIEL ISLANDS

Go left along the road and down the causeway to Roa Island from where the official route begins and this interim stretch ends.

Foulney Island

Walking along through Rampside and down the causeway to Roa you will be aware of the more natural causeway to Foulney Island. This shingle ridge links an SSSI that is famed for its birdlife and flora. Terns are the speciality and the site is wardened. Visitors are discouraged in the breeding season.

It was at Foulney that the legend of the goose barnacle began. These barnacles always seemed to occur in the same places as Barnacle geese. Because of the feathery appearance of the barnacles, the legend grew up that the geese hatched out of them.

Roa Island

Roa Island was once a real island but is now linked to the mainland by a causeway. The first causeway was built in 1847, along with a pier, by John Abel Smith for a steamer service which went to Fleetwood. Rather than pay dues to Smith for using this deep-water harbour to send out iron ore, the railway company built their port at Barrow.

In 1852 the pier was damaged in a storm and the Furness Railway Company purchased Smith's interests for £15000. They rebuilt the pier and causeway, and then used them to carry their rails from the island's steamer pier. From there, iron ore could be shipped out or, in later times, tourists could disembark, board a train and be taken on a tour round the Lakes on the Furness Railway and their lake steamer.

The lifeboat house sits proudly above the waters of Walney Channel a few paces from a house that belonged to Henry Schneider, the Barrow-in-Furness iron dealer. From here you can also catch a small ferry to Piel Island. Ferry times will be found by the jetty.

Piel Island

Piel Island boasts both a castle and a pub, the Ship Inn, whose licensee is 'crowned' King of Piel. The island is a favourite port of call for sailing enthusiasts from the Lancashire Coast as well as for Barrovians. If Piel was near a larger conurbation it would attract many thousands of visitors and lose its feeling of romance. We should therefore be thankful for its remoteness.

Like nearby Walney, Piel was probably formed by deposition from the retreating Duddon glacier. It served as a harbour in early centuries and before that the Vikings may have used it as a grazing island. Later it was granted to Furness Abbey. Baines, in his *History of Lancashire*, quotes from a

The castle on Piel Island is only a short boat trip from Roa Island and the route of the walk.

report of the reign of Queen Elizabeth I, in which it is stated that 'Between Mylford Haven in Wales and Carlisle . . . there is not one good haven for greate shyppes to londe or ryde in but one whiche is in the furthest part of Lancashire called Pylle of Fodder.'

In 1720 the local custom house was at Rampside before it transferred to Ulverston, following a change in the pattern of iron ore shipments. The monks of Furness Abbey gained the land at Rampside along with Piel and its harbour became important to their commercial life. The twelfth-century castle was built by the monks partly as a warehouse. In addition it was intended to guard the entrance to the channel from whence went all their wealth of wool and iron. However its battlements were never completed. It also served as a base for monastic smuggling, as the monks had a taste for fine wine.

Henry IV questioned the monks' right to the castle when they apparently failed to maintain a proper garrison and they in turn feared that the King might put in a revenue officer who would undermine their wool trade. Although they pulled off the roof to make it uninhabitable Henry's men occupied the castle for some time and also took Walney from the monks. However the Abbot regained control and F. Barnes records in *Barrow and District* that in the reign of Henry VI Flemish merchants were using Piel to avoid tax on wool. Tenants of the crown in High Furness had to undertake to man the castle should there be a need to defend the realm.

Much remains of the sandstone fortification, which was reported as ruinous in 1537, but the seaward side has lost some of its grandeur. However the atmosphere is such that you feel the castle ought to be fully restored. The Duke of Buccleuch made some attempt at restoration in 1876–8 and English Heritage carried out further work in the late 1980s.

It was here, on Piel, in 1487 that Lambert Simnel, pretender to the English throne, landed with about 8000 men. After marching via Ulverston and the cross-bay routes Simnel's army was destroyed at Stoke-on-Trent. Piel may also have been the site of a bridgehead of the Spanish Armada.

RAMPSIDE TO BARROW

From here, having been suitably refreshed at the Ship Inn, return by ferry to Roa.

To reach Barrow, walk back along the causeway from Roa towards Rampside. Facing you at the end of the causeway, where the road bends right, is a house which was once the old Rampside station. Go to the right of the house and follow an enclosed track. In so doing you will follow the bed of the railway on what is now part of the Westfield Nature Trail.

When a gate bars your way go left down the enclosed path, then follow it round Westfield Point with the gas terminals to your right. In going round the headland you will leave the old track bed but you will rejoin it on the far side of the first terminal.

At these terminals British Gas collect and treat natural gas from the Morecambe Bay field some 40 km (25 miles) out to sea.

Follow the straight line of the old railway past the Roosecote Power Station and on to reach the edge of Salthouse Pool, pass the new 'sewage' works, and continue ahead.

The spread of Roosecote Sands to your left, particularly as you pass Westfield Point, gives ample opportunities for bird-watching. The rocks of Ridding Head stand out above the flow tide and thus make a favourite roosting place. This area is designated an SSSI largely because of the geological and biological interest of the mudflats, saltmarsh, lagoons, shingle and sand-dune systems. Cavendish Dock and Walney Nature Reserve also come within the designated area.

The power station used to burn an average of 2500 tonnes of coal per week. It was closed in the 1980s but later emerged as a gas-burning, privately operated power station.

Go under the railway bridge and keep left along the Salthouse Road until you emerge near the town centre and the Strand. The town trail (see Chapter 4) begins along here.

CHAPTER 4

BARROW-IN-FURNESS AND WALNEY ISLAND

BARROW

The doyen of Victorian Lake District walkers, M. J. B. Baddeley, wrote: 'Barrow is built on a dead flat, and has, though a well built modern town, nothing to attract the tourist, unless it be large docks and a fine town hall.' These views are often repeated by modern guide book writers and comedians – but Barrow deserves better. Maxwell Fraser came nearer the truth in *Companion into Lakeland* when she said: 'The name of Barrow-in-Furness is to many people a synonym for all that is dreary – most unjustly, for there are many less pleasant places.' Barrow is in fact an attractively situated town, surrounded on three sides by seashore.

The name of the town is taken from Barrow Island which is believed to have been the site of a Norse burial ground. Today the island is the land between Walney Channel and Buccleuch Dock and is largely occupied by VSEL (Vickers Shipbuilding and Engineering Ltd), whose huge submarine-building hall and cranes dominate the skyline for miles around.

At the end of the eighteenth century the village of Barrowhead had around 300 souls but all changed after the building of three jetties to ship out Furness iron ore. With the input of local landowners, whose names can still be recognised in local place names, and Henry Schneider – a speculator and dealer in iron – the town's prosperity grew. The coming of the Furness Railway, in 1846, gave added impetus to Barrow's development, much of which was due to the work of the locomotive superintendent James Ramsden.

The first major dock, the Devonshire, opened in 1867. (The Duke of Devonshire, like Buccleuch, was a major landowner.) Barrow thus grew rapidly, aiming to become a second Liverpool. Both landowners backed Ramsden's plan for the town, based on industrial land near the docks and housing areas further inland linked by tree-lined streets.

Iron ore was being shipped out as early as 1745 from the beach and a quay was made in 1782 to cope with the increasing quantities being handled. By 1833 there were two jetties and further piers were added in 1839 and 1842. However economic success was still not guaranteed.

In 1850 Schneider stumbled over the vast Park deposits of iron ore north of Barrow, near Askam. By 1857 the railway had been connected to the main London–Glasgow route and blast furnaces had been erected. It was around this time that Ramsden started planning the new town of Barrow.

Iron

The iron industry has a much older history in the area and there are several Roman and monastic iron bloomery sites to be found in the Lake District. The presence of iron ore, sometimes in very rich haematite deposits, started the process of industrial development in many of the towns along the Coastal Way. However it wasn't until 1735 that blast furnaces with coke came into common use and industry began to develop along the shores of Cumbria.

The existence of the bloomeries led to the establishment of many early furnaces, mostly near water and woodland because transporting iron ore to the charcoal and bloomery was the most economically effective method. A traditional bloomery might make 1.5 tons of iron a year but in so doing would need to use 9 hectares (22 acres) of woodland.

In the nineteenth century the iron industry expanded enormously. Whilst most mines had closed after the end of the Great War, some – like Hodbarrow, and others to the north – continued until later this century. There were in essence two separate ore fields – the more compact Furness area and the more extensive Cumberland field. Both fields produced non-phosphoric haematite ore with very high iron content, sometimes as high as 60 per cent iron.

Although the ore was not too deep down it was usually mined. Some of the deposits were massive flats or accumulations which left huge cavities, especially in Furness. As in coal mines, the ingress of water was a problem.

By 1876 Barrow could claim to have the world's largest ironworks. The local iron-rich haematite gave the area a huge advantage when the Bessemer steel-making process was developed. But, once the process had been adapted to use phosphor-containing ores, these natural advantages were lost and there were more successful developments elsewhere. The steelworks finally closed in 1983. It was another local industry, shipbuilding (which had begun a few years earlier) that was to form the basis of the town's future prosperity. To a large extent, it still does so today.

Railways

The railways were a natural development from the system of coal wagonways that served both the coal and iron ore fields. The major railways along the coast were created mainly after 1840. It was at one time proposed, by George Stephenson, that the main line to Scotland should take a coastal route rather than the line over Shap which opened in 1846. The railway now forms an important backbone to the walk from Silverdale/Arnside to Maryport and Carlisle.

The link from Maryport to Carlisle, giving manufacturers an outlet to the sea and enabling the mineral wealth of the coastal area to reach Carlisle, was a major factor in the development of the coastal system. This latter railway was opened, as a single track, in 1845–6, with a proposed continuation to run south along the coast to the Furness system, around Barrow, and back to the main Lancaster and Carlisle line at Carnforth. However, in the event, the development of the coastal line was more piecemeal, with separate companies linking together and eventually joining in the Furness railway system at Broughton-in-Furness in 1850.

Inter-railway rivalry was intense, but it was the London and

North-Western Railway that always dominated the north-western corner of England. Nevertheless some companies, like the Furness and the Cleator and Whitehaven, remained independent of this giant – largely because their mineral traffic made them very profitable.

Nowadays the Barrow ironworks and many of the railways have gone. Even so, the slagbank, though being dismantled, still dominates the town's northern seaboard. Industry has diversified – there is the gas terminal from the Morecambe Bay field, toilet tissue, chemicals – but it is ships, especially submarines, which are regarded as the real barometer of the town's economic health.

A Barrow Town Trail

To the right, on Salthouse Road, lies a small terrace of cottages built for railway workers in local red sandstone in 1846. When they were constructed they increased the number of houses in Barrow by about 25 per cent!

St George's Church nearby is one of the few buildings in Barrow made from Lakeland green slate. The south chapel is called the Ramsden Chapel.

The Strand was intended to be the town centre in Ramsden's plan and to your left, by the dock road, was the original Barrow railway station. The warehouse on Devonshire dock is a massive piece of mid-nineteenth-century architecture.

Go down the grandly named Strand, to Michaelson Road and then Schneider Square – with its statue of Henry Schneider. Turn right and follow Dalton Road through the shopping centre to arrive at Abbey Road.

As you go down Abbey Road, one of Ramsden's tree-lined streets, you will see a series of solid, individual, grand-looking buildings – including the Conservative Club and, at Ramsden Square, the library.

After reaching Ramsden Square, continue down Duke Street.

The statue of Ramsden, dated 1872, has an interesting plaque depicting the industrial foundation of the town.

Off Duke Street you can see largely unaltered grid-patterned streets of terraced houses. Duke Street itself has some attractive examples of moulded brickwork from the 1860s and 1870s if you look above shop level. The terraces of houses arranged in and around the town centre enable Barrow's residents to live close to their central amenities. Unlike many towns in the north-west, with their uninhabited centres, Barrow still has a heart. The terraces behind the shops on the right of Duke Street are especially good examples of nineteenth-century artisans' dwellings.

The Town Hall was completed in 1882. It is of classic Victorian Gothic style and crowned with a high clock tower, though the symmetry is spoilt by the council chamber having four windows. Tours are sometimes available. Do not miss the stained glass window or the climb to the tower. The main entrance, a *porte cochere*, is at the rear, giving the hall a strange inverted feeling. Inside the red sandstone and slate-roofed building, there is an almost Dickensian atmosphere.

From outside the Town Hall a no. 6 bus will take you to see the superb sandstone ruins of Furness Abbey.

From the Town Hall, go back up Duke Street to Ramsden Square and turn left by the roundabout into Hindpool Road. Turn right, cross the road and then go left down North Road to reach Devonshire Bridge where the now entombed Devonshire Dock once led out to Walney Channel. If you intend to explore Walney, go straight ahead into Bridge Road and turn right to reach Jubilee Bridge. If you want to press on north towards the Duddon estuary, cross North Road on the near side of Devonshire Bridge. The prestigious Dock Museum is beside the bridge.

WALNEY ISLAND

The rest of this chapter is included for those who want to spend a day exploring Walney Island. The route is waymarked as part of the Cumbria Coastal Way.

Walney Island is some 13 km (8 miles) long and never quite 2 km (1¼ mile) wide. The southernmost land in the county of Cumbria, it was occupied by Mesolithic hunter-fisherman after the ice age. The island is itself an esker, a remnant of the retreating Duddon glacier.

Archaeological finds have included flints used for barbs of harpoons and arrowheads, and scrapers and knives used to catch and skin animals and carve wood and bone. Some of the axes were made from pebbles found in local boulder clay cliffs, whilst others came from the Neolithic traffic of rough-hewn Lakeland axeheads some 3000 years ago.

The main axe factory site was at North End but remains of Mesolithic and Beaker peoples have been found elsewhere on the island. This site was in use something like 5000 years ago and involved trade with Ireland as well as the more central Lake District.

The name Walney appears to have been derived from 'walled island', either referring to the walls of stones pushed up the beaches by the sea or to the walls built by early settlers.

By the mid-thirteenth century Furness Abbey had three grange farms on the island. The abbey undertook some drainage work and a protective dyke, originally built under the auspices of the monks, can be seen north of Biggar.

Today parts of the island suffer from the disadvantages of poorly maintained field boundaries, difficult farming conditions, over-conspicuous caravan sites and rubbish tipping. Against this, you have the interest of the old smugglers' village of Biggar, two important nature reserves and the Vickerstown Conservation Area, all of which make the island worth visiting for a day. Check the bus routes in Barrow if you wish to take this alternative loop to the main walk. Buses 1 and 2 go to Walney (south and north respectively). There is also a lagoon on the coast of the island where, at any one time, fifteen million oysters are being reared for a worldwide market.

To reach Walney Island, walk from Devonshire Bridge down North Road and turn right to reach Vickerstown via Jubilee Bridge.

Jubilee Bridge was built to replace the ferry that served the then growing settlement of Vickerstown. Beginning life as as toll bridge in 1908, it was made free of charge in 1935. The aging structure is, in part, a swing bridge but large vessels rarely use this upper part of Walney Channel nowadays.

The South Walney Nature Reserve
This SSSI is at the southernmost tip of the island. Once an area of mineral workings, it is now the largest breeding site in Europe for lesser black-backed and herring gulls. There are also ring plovers, roseate terns and eider ducks. The shingle flora and the erosional and depositional features on the beach add further interest. The site is permanently wardened by the Cumbria Wildlife Trust. Admission is by permit only and this can be obtained at the warden's house next to the reserve any day apart from Mondays (Bank Holidays excepted). May and June are the best times to visit.

The Trinity House Lighthouse
The Trinity House lighthouse on South End Haws was built for £1000 in 1799 and guides shipping from Morecambe Bay by way of Walney to Barrow docks. This listed building is not open to the public.

Biggar
The hamlet of Biggar is a compact, introspective-looking settlement. Local building materials – cobble walls or rough-cast facing and slate roofs – together with the layout of the hamlet add to the feeling of a sheltered haven and, perhaps, secrecy and smuggling. Inside the hamlet change is taking place, old agricultural barns are becoming homes, and Biggar's history and character are gradually being destroyed. However if you wander around the small village you will see a number of lovely old buildings, including Town End Farm, New Inn, Manor Farmhouse, Hill Farm, Piel View Farm and the Queen's Arms.

Just outside Biggar is Biggar Dyke. This embankment was constructed by the monks of Furness Abbey to protect their adjacent fields from the tides. After the Dissolution the tenants were given reduced rents in return for maintaining the dyke. However some of them neglected their duties and there are court records of tenants being fined for not providing their share of labour.

The other area of importance for natural history is the north tip of the island – Walney North End SSSI – which lies beyond the airfield. If you wish to visit the area, which includes many interesting plants and the rare natterjack toad, a permit should be obtained from VSEL (see Useful Addresses).

Just off North End is Scarth Hole, a permanent stretch of water which holds some interesting marine life. This includes an Australian barnacle which apparently reached Scarth Hole on the bottom of World War II convoy ships.

Vickerstown
Just west of the bridge and promenade is Vickerstown Conservation Area. This settlement was conceived as a private housing venture by the Isle of Walney Estate Company as part of the overall development of the island as a resort and in conjunction with a substantial expansion of the shipbuilding facilities across the channel. When the company found itself in financial difficulties Vickers took them over and proceeded to build the estate on the lines of Port Sunlight (the pioneering Lever Brothers village on the Wirral). Between 1899 and 1904 nearly 4000 houses, a bowling green, an institute reading room and a park were constructed.

The streets were spacious but the houses were cheaply built, with pebbledash render and timber-framed gables, and the site lacked the attractive landscaping of Port Sunlight. The streets were named after ships built at Barrow and after famous admirals. Many are still maintained with pride – hence the Conservation Area accolade. The area behind the school, in particular, is well worth a visit with its Powerful and Melampus Streets.

North Scale
North Scale is one of Walney's older settlements. Some of its
houses have seventeenth-century date stones and provide
interesting examples of vernacular architecture. They are
built of stones gathered from the foreshore and rendered.

WALNEY TO THE MAINLAND
Several fords once linked the island to the mainland and
Barrow Island but these were mostly lost when Barrow began
to expand. One ford, between North Scale and Hindpool, is
marked by a concrete footbridge seen at low tide. This was
originally built in 1860 to replace the worn stepping stones of
the adjacent 'Low Steps'. Another, further north, while still a
public right of way, required a tunnel under the slagbanks to
give people access to the ford.

The channel between Walney and Barrow is full of
glutinous mud and cockle beds. Going back to Jubilee
Bridge, we can retrace our steps to Devonshire Bridge to
continue along the Way.

At low tide the old walkway across Walney Channel is
revealed.

SECTION TWO
THE DUDDON ESTUARY

CHAPTER 5

**BARROW-IN-FURNESS TO
BROUGHTON-IN-FURNESS
23 km (14 miles)**

CHAPTER 6

**BROUGHTON-IN-FURNESS TO MILLOM AND
SILECROFT
23 km (14 miles)**

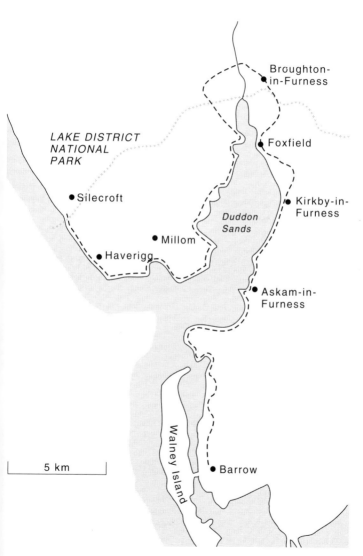

Broughton-in-Furness

Foxfield

LAKE DISTRICT
NATIONAL
PARK

Silecroft

Kirkby-in-Furness

Duddon
Sands

Millom

Haverigg

Askam-in-Furness

Walney Island

5 km

Barrow

61

The Duddon estuary is one of the few genuinely wild, romantic places of the British countryside. The different combinations of sun and tide cause myriad changes of light, culminating in wonderful sunsets and beautiful reflections from wet sand and river channel. Sadly, proposals are currently being considered to dam, or bridge, this superb estuary in order to generate electrical power and link Barrow and Millom.

The estuary originated when the dome of Lakeland rocks was etched by rivers, including, along a fault line, the Duddon. Then came the ice age and the glaciers that deeply cut its bed. As the area warmed up the sea level rose and flooded the over-deepened river valley, turning it into an estuary. Gradually, over the last 10000 years, the ice and water have further sculpted the fells and contributed to the silting of the estuary.

Whilst the Way takes us over recently laid down sediments, it is the oldest rocks of the area, the Skiddaw Slates (formed under the sea) which form the mass of Black Combe. This fell dominates the route for much of the southern part of the walk. The Duddon estuary received many of the Norse immigrants who came by way of Ireland, the Isle of Man or Scotland in the tenth century. Doubtless the bulk of Black Combe provided them with their beacon.

The Duddon rises high above Wrynose Pass and before 1974 it formed the boundary between Lancashire's High Furness and Cumberland. This boundary had existed since William II gave Furness to a powerful Norman earl, Roger of Poitou, in 1092. At other times the river has formed the boundary between England and Strathclyde.

The Duddon was once a source of cockles that were not only abundant but said to be the finest available. Local people also gathered salmon and today the river is well known for its sea trout.

The estuary has many old roads marked across it on the Ordnance Survey map. However, unlike the Kent and Leven sands, it never had a salaried guide although a local inn did provide a sand pilot on request.

Norman Nicholson, who lived in Millom and died in 1986, wrote a poem called 'To the River Duddon' which catches the spirit of the estuary very well. The Duddon was also one of Wordsworth's favourite rivers and he wrote a sequence of 34 Duddon Sonnets, in which he traced the river from source to sea, from birth to death:

> Not hurled precipitous from steep to steep;
> Lingering no more 'mid flowering-enamelled lands
> And blooming thickets; nor by rocky bands
> Heed; but in radiant progress toward the Deep
> Where mightiest rivers into powerless sleep
> Sink, and forget their nature – now expands
> Majestic Duddon, over smooth flat sands
> Gliding in silence with unfettered sweep!
> Beneath an ampler sky a region wide
> Is opened round him: – hamlets, towers and towns,
> And blue topped hills, behold him from afar . . .

The rocky outcrop of Dunnerholme juts into the Duddon Estuary, with Millom and Black Combe over the sands.

CHAPTER 5

BARROW-IN-FURNESS TO BROUGHTON-IN FURNESS

BARROW TO ASKAM

From Devonshire Bridge proceed along Bridge Road to the Dock Museum (see Chapter 4). When work on the slagbanks has been completed the Coastal Way should be diverted along the side of the channel. Until then, go up North Road to the T-junction, left into Hindpool Road, and continue past the former ironworks offices into Walney Road.

It may not be a pleasant idea to walk along the edge of a huge slagbank but already the sound and feel of the sea is there, and you will see some fascinating reminders of Barrow's industrial past. The earlist converter from the former ironworks is apparently exhibited in London's Science Museum. A tunnel, which once gave access to a ford, was situated halfway along. For interesting information on the history of the ironworks, refer to A. G. Banks' book *H. W. Schneider of Barrow and Bowness*.

Walney Road crosses the railway, becomes Ormsgill Lane and brings you to a crossroads. Go left along Park Road and after the last house on the right and the end of a row of factories on the left, look for a path off to your left (signed to Sowerby Lodge). (This part of the route is covered by **Way Map 4**.) Go through the stile between gates, follow the left-hand hedge down the field and cross the gated

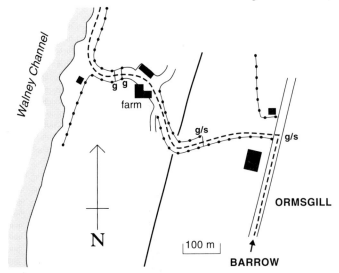

Way Map 4: Route by Sowerby Lodge Farm, Barrow

railway bridge. Continue along the track to the farm, turn left through the yard, leave by the double gates and continue down an enclosed track to the shore.

Once on the coast, follow the waymarked path right and around Scarth Bight. Continue round the sands to pass Lowsy Point, some think aptly named, until you eventually arrive at Roanhead. At very high tides, cut across between the dunes and fields to Roanhead. Do not go over the dunes or across the fields themselves.

The tidal bay of Scarth Bight provides a backdrop for flights of shelduck and feeding oystercatchers. The public right of way crosses the middle of the bay but proves to be a glutinous trudge. The waymarked path round the edge of dry land is better. Between the north end of Walney and the jutting peninsula of Sandscale Haws you will glimpse Millom and Black Combe – looking tantalisingly close.

Sandscale Haws SSSI

Sandscale Haws is designated an SSSI because of its interesting flora and fauna. Natterjack toads, some 15 per cent of the British population, live in some of the pools. One pool, fed by a stream due to the loss of pools in dry years, has a board walk so that visitors can enjoy watching the antics of the toads and their tadpoles. There are several hundred plant and animal species and several will be seen from your route along the beach. Protected orchids grow on the dunes, along with creeping willow, harebell, lady's bedstraw and thyme. The National Trust produce an excellent leaflet on the area which should be read before you pass through. It is available from the National Trust or Barrow-in-Furness Tourist Information Centre (see Useful Addresses).

Roanhead

A small terrace of houses by the car park and a refreshment cabin/shop mark Roanhead. This is where Barrow goes to the seaside, especially on sunny Thursdays (half-day closing). Along the shore from Roanhead to Askam are several waterlogged holes used by fisherfolk. The red, barren margins are the remains of long-abandoned haematite mines, the source of the area's prosperity. The fabulous Park mine lies higher above the shore.

The story goes that Henry Schneider visited the Lakes in 1839 and was shown a small iron ore mine at Askam. A year later he returned to take a lease on the area from the Earl of Burlington (later the Duke of Devonshire). Ten years later, on the point of abandoning his project, Schneider discovered the richest lode of haematite then known in Britain. Only later did Hodbarrow (after Millom on the Coastal Way) excel Park which produced some 7 million tonnes of finest-quality ore between 1850 and 1922.

Continue along the foreshore from Roanhead to reach Askam.

66

Askam

The first sign of Askam-in-Furness is the 'Pier' that looks like a futile attempt to dam the Duddon. In fact it merely provided a way of depositing slag from the local ironworks – in the direction of Millom. The ironworks closed in 1918, having had its life prolonged by the Great War. The plant had four Bessemer converters planned to make steel but financial problems prevented the realisation of this dream. The works lay derelict until they were demolished in 1933–4.

Askam is a small industrial town where back-to-back houses line grid-plan streets with names like Foundry Road. The town was never completed, as shown by gaps in the grids of older terraces, and even the plans to become a Victorian seaside town came to nought.

Until 1865 this area was simply marshy open country beside the estuary, and neighbouring rabbit warrens. In 1864 there was a plan to bridge the estuary for the railway and now, in the 1990s, philistines are contemplating a barrage and a bridge.

ASKAM TO KIRKBY

It is tempting to think that Millom lies only a short stroll over the sands of the Duddon estuary. Indeed a 'public road' does go this way, but the time between tides is shorter here than further up the estuary and drowning incidents are not unknown. When Millom was expanding in the last century those who perished here were often those who came to look for employment and were, to quote William Palmer, 'mostly out of work and others with little strength to fight against storm and fog and menacing waters.'

> Continue along the shoreline to reach the right-hand edge of the limestone cliffs of Dunnerholme which project into the estuary, with the golf course to your right. (See **Way Map 5**.)

Dunnerholme

Dunnerholme is a small but impressive limestone finger that juts into the estuary. Together with St Bees Head and

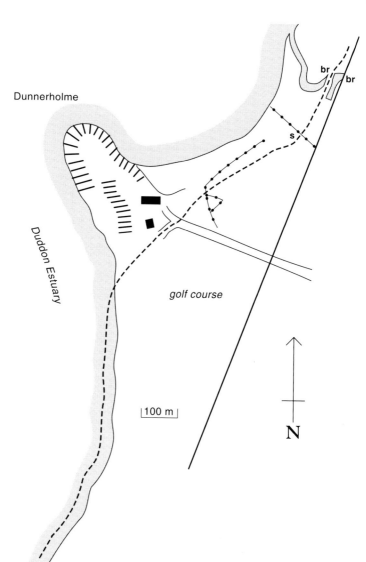

Dunnerholme

Duddon Estuary

golf course

br
br

s

100 m

N

Way Map 5: Dunnerholme Cliffs and Duddon Estuary
68

Humphrey Head, it is one of only three major rock cliffs on the Cumbrian coast. It is worth stopping here for a while, if only to shelter from the breeze and enjoy the view.

In the foreground the weathered quarry and the elevated golf tee of the holme give way to the sea and the sands, while the wonderful backdrop of Lakeland fells includes Black Combe, Scafell Pikes and Scafell and the Coniston fells.

Between the golf course and the railway line are a series of wet slacks, one of several places along the Way where you may see – or, more likely, hear – the natterjack toad.

Just over the railway line from Dunnerholme lies Marsh Grange Farm. The house is late seventeenth century 'with wooden cross windows and a pair of gate piers too grand for it', according to Nikolaus Pevsner, author of *Buildings of England* (North Lancashire). He classifies the gate piers as 'all very English Baroque'. The farm site was previously a grange farm owned by Furness Abbey.

From Dunnerholme go to the left-hand side of an enclosed tee, cross the remainder of the golf course, parallel to the railway, and continue along the foundations of an old wall. Cross the fence by the stile, then go straight ahead and cross the footbridge over the dyke. From here, continue north, making the best of the grass between the reeds (the way is far from smooth) to Kirkby-in-Furness railway station. Here Kirkby Pool flows into the Duddon on your left. Part of this way is permissive and dogs *must* be kept on a lead. Very high tides wash the saltmarsh.

The Duddon-side Marshes

The saltmarshes are grazed by sheep but these animals are moved to safer pastures when higher tides cover the grass. Cumbria is famous for its sea-washed turf, prized by gardeners and footballers alike.

Birds nest in hollows and sea pinks are a feature of the Duddon-side marshes. (*Beware of high tides rising up the gullies and over the turf* if no grazing is taking place.) In the winter, when flocks of geese home in on the saltings, joining large flocks of lapwings and godwits, these areas become even more magical.

> Kirkby station is opposite the Ship Inn in the settlement called Sandside. Cross by the footbridge and go left down the road. Continue until the road bends sharp right where the houses of Marshside begin.

Kirkby-in-Furness

The small hamlets which make up the village of Kirkby-in-Furness are overshadowed by massive slate quarries and windmills on the fellside above. The moors, on which the quarries are situated, are composed of Silurian rocks and reach an altitude of over 300 m (1000 ft).

The quarrying began in earnest in 1771 when Lord John Cavendish purchased the manor. Even though Kirkby-in-Furness was then in Lancashire the slate was known as Westmorland Dark Blue. William Cavendish (1809–1891) became Earl of Burlington and the quarries are still named after him. Kirkby 'Roundhead' and other varieties of slates were used on the roofs of back-to-back houses throughout the north-west during the industrial revolution.

An inclined railway, the route of which can still be followed, was built to join the Furness Railway. Before this, the slate had been shipped out from Kirkby Pool, Angerton and Ulverston. Coniston copper was once shipped from near Kirkby station, to be refined at St Helens. The line of the incline railway, crossed on the road from the station, passes close to Kirkby Hall, a sixteenth-century manor house with some curious frescoes in the loft, formerly a chapel.

Across from the Ship Inn at Sandside, there is a house (originally a barn) with some unusual examples of nineteenth-century carving. Do the curious inscriptions indicate that the mason indulged in frequent visits to the inn opposite?

Higher up in the village, at Beckside, the church dedicated to St Cuthbert has several points of interest and is especially worth seeing in springtime when crocus and dog violet clothe the graveyard.

KIRKBY TO BROUGHTON

At Marshside, leave the road to the left of the first house and enter the field by the stile. Follow the right-hand boundary initially but then keep to the left of the overhead wires to reach and cross a stile. Go left down the track, through the yard of Moss Houses Farm, and then turn right at the road junction beyond. Follow this lane as it bends left, passes Waitham Wood, climbs to pass Waitham Hill Farm and then descends to cross the mossland of Waitham Common in a dead straight line. The road then bends left, crosses the railway, follows it right and recrosses the line at Foxfield.

Waitham Comman

Waitham Common forms part of the Duddon Mosses SSSI. After those of the Solway Plain, these eight mosses are the most important lowland raised mires in Great Britain because of their size and diversity of habitats. The mosses support typical bog communities of plants, along with heather, scrub and some woodland. Deer and adders have also been seen.

Over the Foxfield crossing, go left (towards the station and pub) and take the first lane off to the right. This surfaced lane climbs, goes through three gates and then through the yard of Coal Gate Farm. (This part of the route is shown on **Way Map 6**.) Leave the yard by a further gate, go along the lane and through the first field gate on your left. Follow the wall down the field, go through the gate facing you and continue, with the wall on your right. Cross this wall by the second gate, turn left and descend to cross the stile in the corner of the field.

Cross the next (narrow) field, go over the footbridge, turn half-right, and climb the short bank by the second large sycamore. Continue directly up the bank over the golf course to a shallow track. Follow the track ahead and when it bends right continue directly ahead to reach a small wood. Pass through the wood and go ahead to a lane by some cottages.

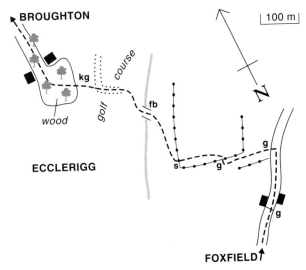

Way Map 6: Foxfield to Broughton

Follow the lane until you emerge on the road just above Broughton-in-Furness. Turn left and drop down to the village, with the village square straight ahead.

Broughton

Broughton-in-Furness is thought to be Old English for 'settlement by a brook'. The church dates from the eleventh century and has Saxon walls and a Norman archway. To the north of the village lies Broughton Tower which originated as a twelfth-century Norman keep.

The attractive square is often obscured by parked cars but the obelisk (commemorating the fiftieth year of the reign of George III) and the stocks help Broughton retain its eighteenth-century market town atmosphere. There are several good hostelries and eating places in the village.

CHAPTER 6

BROUGHTON-IN-FURNESS TO MILLOM AND SILECROFT

From the left-hand corner of Broughton Square, go down Griffin Street, keep right at the Old King's Head and walk up the Millom road. Turn right at the junction by High Cross and go down the main road. Just before the road crosses the River Lickle, at the end of the left-hand wall, go left to follow an enclosed path over a footbridge, and continue by the right-hand boundary until you reach a gate by the river. Through the gate, follow the riverside track, past the old quay, to reach the road at Duddon Bridge. Cross this road with care.

Broughton-in-Furness, a recommended overnight stop.

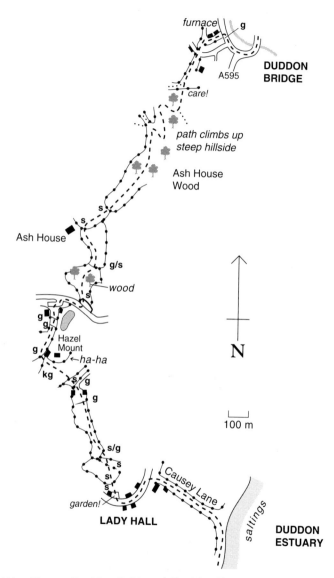

Way Map 7: Duddon Bridge to Duddon Estuary

DUDDON BRIDGE TO MILLOM

From Duddon Bridge to between Whitehaven and Working-ton the route passes through the borough of Copeland. The name was taken from the old Norse name for the area. *Kaupland*, which means 'bought land', though we may never know who the vendor and Norse purchaser were.

The Scandinavians were seen as pirates, arriving by way of Scotland, Ireland and the Isle of Man in the ninth century. Eventually they settled and played a formative role in the history of the area. Norse place names still dominate the map of Cumbria today, as do many dialect words still in common usage. The Norse people may have been encouraged to settle in some coastal areas by the local kings and their more professional soldiers probably helped to reinforce the coastal defences.

The Scandinavian farmers are believed to have preferred upland pastures but there is also evidence that they took arable land which was not being fully utilised. Eventually they became the dominant landowners. In some cases they are thought to have used force to get rid of the original land-owners. In other cases the Norsemen may have purchased estates such as Copeland. Palaeobiological evidence from pollen deposits suggests that there was a great deal of tree clearance around this time, implying that more land was being brought into cultivation.

The Norse people created new farmlands from the wilder uplands, probably using them as summer pastures and the way they ran their estates almost certainly laid down the pattern for the estates, hunting chases and parish boundaries of the Normans. The present borough boundary is very close to that of the Norman baronial hunting forest of Copeland, which was once a refuge for deer, wolves and wild boar. The area became a baronry in 1120 when Ranulf de Briquessart granted the lands to his brother William Meschines. Egremont was then its administrative centre.

The borough now boasts England's highest peaks, Scafell Pikes and Scafell, and it also contains its deepest lake, Wastwater.

The Duddon Iron Furnace

The Duddon iron furnace was one of eight charcoal-fired blast furnaces set up in the southern Lakes in the early eighteenth century. The site was adjacent to charcoal-producing woodlands, not far from a supply of iron ore, and could provide water power for the furnace bellows. Dating from 1736–7, this furnace was working until 1867. The site has been extensively restored by the Lake District National Park Authority.

The charcoal-fired iron furnace at Duddon Bridge.

To reach the furnace, go over Duddon Bridge and right at the junction. After about 100 m (110 yds) you will see the furnace on your left. Take care if you follow the road to Lady Hall.

The official route from Duddon Bridge to the railway viaduct is still under development and **Way Map 7** suggests a route we have taken in order to bypass this section. You can follow it on your O.S. sheet, Pathfinder 625.

From Lady Hall go down Causey Lane and follow the track to the right until you reach the railway embankment through a gate. Continue on the track but, just short of the next gate, turn left to cross the railway by a pair of stiles. Rejoin the embankment by a further stile to the left. Follow this along, with High Shaw Farm inland. Come down to the farm access track, cross the inlet stream and then rejoin the embankment to continue around the edge of the saltings. This route gives an elevated view of the estuary all the way to the edge of Millom.

Swinside Stone Circle

On Duddon's west bank, high above the Green Road station, lies Swinside stone circle. Over 2000 years old, the 50 stones form a circle of about 30 m (100 ft) in diameter which is known locally as Sunkenkirk. If you have time and energy to spare, it is well worth a visit. See Pathfinder Map 625 for directions.

The saltmarsh provides grazing for sheep and, alas, targets for those who enjoy shooting wildfowl. It was by these marshes that greylag geese were successfully reintroduced into Cumbria.

Ahead lies the tempting beacon of Millom's St George's church tower which finally seems to be getting closer.

The embankment, where Millom folk once paraded on Sundays, continues round a small inlet stream, goes through the pillars of the old railway line to the ironworks, and enters the streets of Millom.

Millom

The slagbanks and pigeon lofts welcome you. In many ways they tell the history of Millom, a town that exists because of iron. It collapsed economically and socially when the mines and furnaces closed in 1968 but since then it has fought back to regain a higher rate of employment and economic activity.

The original settlement was on Holborn Hill, above the railway. Those buildings below the rails are Newtown, an industrial settlement of slate-built houses constructed on former dunes, saltmarsh and swampy fields in 1866.

Just outside the town stand the massive remains of Millom

Castle which is now part of a farmhouse. The castle was built in the fourteenth century to guard the ford over the Duddon. After suffering a raid by the Scots in 1322 it was rebuilt, and in 1335 Sir John Huddleston enclosed his house and church by moat and added battlements to the house.

The castle had to be restored again in 1460 after damage sustained in the Wars of the Roses (for the Huddlestons were Yorkists). Later, in 1644, during the Civil War, the castle was besieged by Parliamentary forces. Millom Castle is not normally open to the public but you can ask for permission at the farmhouse.

The history of the castle and church are interwined through the ownership of the Huddleston family. Holy Trinity, a late Norman building on an earlier foundation, is built of the local red sandstone. A south aisle was added in the thirteenth century and the interestingly shaped west window has nineteenth-century tracery. The pews are boxed and the snug but light and spacious church retains a great deal of its ancient charm despite many restorations.

Next to the track on the landward side of the railway lies a weather-beaten block of sandstone whose inscription reads 'Here the Lords of Millom exercised Julia Regalia', the power of life or death over their tenants. In short, they were hanged here at their Lordships' pleasure. The stone was positioned by the landward end of the usual cross-sands route to the castle. Alas, time and neglect have almost eaten away the inscription.

In Millom itself the church of St George's central tower and recessed spire is a dominant landmark. The avenue of limes leading to the church was funded by local nineteenth-century iron barons.

The Millom Folk Museum, just behind the library, is worth a visit for it tells us more about the iron industry which so strongly influences the next few kilometres of the walk. The library is named in memory of Norman Nicholson who drew so much on Black Combe, Millom and the Duddon in his highly acclaimed poetry, which is a unique combination of topography, nature and elements of his Christian faith.

Norman Nicholson lived all his life in Millom, apart from a period of exile in a TB sanatorium. His novels he preferred to forget, his plays are hardly seen but his poetry and topographical writings can take their place beside those of Wordsworth at his best. Some of his older works are now out of print but Faber & Faber publish his *Selected Poems* and local author Irvine Hunt has compiled an illustrated anthology of Nicholson's prose (published by Hale).

MILLOM TO SILECROFT

The official route turns left before the abuttments of the former railway bridge as you leave the embankment to enter Millom, and goes round the track bed of the former ironworks railway line, between the slagbanks. It then turns right and inshore, by the former ironworks pier (now a ship breaker's yard), to reach the road junction. The old ironworks site is to the right. Alternatively, if you wish to visit the museum and town centre, go straight along Lancashire Road as you enter the town, and left down Devonshire Road to rejoin the official route at the gate of the track to the waste water treatment works.

In the 1960s we remember sitting outside an old quarry building high on Coniston Old Man at night and watching the distant plumes of orange flame spewing into the darkness from Millom blast furnaces. That was before 1968 when the furnaces finally cooled and the nearby Hodbarrow mines became inundated with water.

Now the works are long gone, and only slagbanks remain. A new lake occupies the hollow in the reclaimed land where miners once sought riches from the earth.

The ironworks and mines shipped out their products from Borwick Rails harbour. Though the long quay is now decaying it is still an evocative sight. It has served Duddon ships since the 1750s. Until around 1920 it was also the setting for the local regatta. Now used for ship breaking and sometimes as a port, the quay gives wonderful views up the estuary towards the Scafells and Coniston fells.

Go left through the gate, pass the waste water treatment plant, continue through the small gate ahead and then climb the stile in the left-hand corner of the field ahead. Cross the rocky causeway of Salthouse Pool and follow the track ahead to reach the remains of Borwick Rails quay.

Climb a further stile, turn right, pass the pole where the under-estuary cable comes ashore, and go along the seaward edge of the long field. Pass a ruin, and continue until a small wall forces you on to the foreshore. Turn right immediately beyond the wall, pass through a small gate and go left up the path to pass the right-hand side of the windmill. Go downhill, and then left on the track to follow the arc of the barrier to your left.

Hodbarrow Mines

The Hodbarrow mines, before their closure in 1968, were the most productive iron ore mines in the world. The ore is found in the limestone rock that continues under the Duddon estuary into Furness and, geologically, links us with the earlier stages of the walk.

The ore deposits were discovered here in 1843 by the Earl of Lonsdale but large-scale extraction only began after he had leased the rights in 1855. Rich deposits, some 30 m (100 ft) thick, were discovered. The old windmill, which we pass, served as the first company offices, adjacent to Towsey Hole, the first mine. At the height of their prosperity these mines employed 2000 people.

The outer barrier was actually the third, built in 1888–9 to protect the mines from the sea. The second eventually collapsed; both had permitted extension of the mines under the sea.

When Hodbarrow closed the pumping system was switched off, allowing first the mines and then the hollow to flood. A metal lighthouse was built to replace the redundant stone one on the middle barrier.

In 1978 planning permission was given for a huge holiday development on the site around the hollow. It had little success and changed hands in the late 1980s. Around this time

The iron lighthouse at the former Hodbarrow iron mines.

the Royal Society for the Protection of Birds gained an interest in the site and turned most of it into a nature reserve. Terns are a particular feature, whilst natterjack toads also spawn around the edges of Cumbria's newest lake.

Continue past the iron lighthouse, turn left at the end of the embankment, and continue round the edge of the sea defences to reach the River Lazy at Haverigg. Cross the bridge, go left to the front and then continue along the top of the sea defence until it comes to an end by the first sand dune.

Lacra Bronze Age Settlement

Inland, on a minor ridge before Black Combe, lies Lacra with its series of stone circles and what appear to be relics of two avenues of standing stones – the remains of a Bronze Age settlement.

From the first dune follow the coast until you arrive at Silecroft. The walk will be on smooth sand accompanied by the calls of sea birds, if you can time your arrival for low tide. If not, you will be on leg-tiring loose shingle. Watch out for the flowers by the shingle and dunes.

Shingle beaches are very difficult areas for plants to put down roots on, because the loose stones are always in motion. On the higher reaches of shingle beaches, however, you might find the yellow-horned poppy or sea holly, as well as a few smaller species. Turnstones and oystercatchers frequent these areas, particularly when the muddy beaches are covered in water. Washed-up crabs and other invertebrates provide food for ringed plovers, whilst dunlins and turnstones feed lower down the beach.

Sand dunes are also important habitats, especially at Sandscale Haws, along the raised beaches north of Maryport, and between Allonby and Silloth. Once the sand has been stabilised by plants such as marram grass, other species can start to colonise. The resulting dunes also provide habitats for

Low tide at Haverigg.

nesting birds and rare species such as the natterjack toad and some orchids. These habitats can easily be damaged by trampling – please keep to the path.

Once you round Haverigg Point, which seems so close to Barrow, you have really turned the corner to head north. We make no apologies for the circuitous route, for it has enabled us to share with you one of our favourite corners of England. Now the Irish Sea will accompany us to the Solway.

Just over the sand dunes, on the former airfield that houses Haverigg Prison, is a wind farm erected in 1992. Haverigg is also the site of a prehistoric midden where archaeologists have found shells of oysters, winkles, mussels, cockles and limpets, along with a pelican's foot, showing the importance of the sea in providing food for the local ancient Britons.

Along the coastal stretch toward Silecroft we cross the invisible boundary into the Lake District National Park, a parish boundary that also marks the end of the Duddon and the start of a relatively unknown but fascinating part of Lakeland.

SECTION THREE
THE
LAKE DISTRICT
NATIONAL PARK

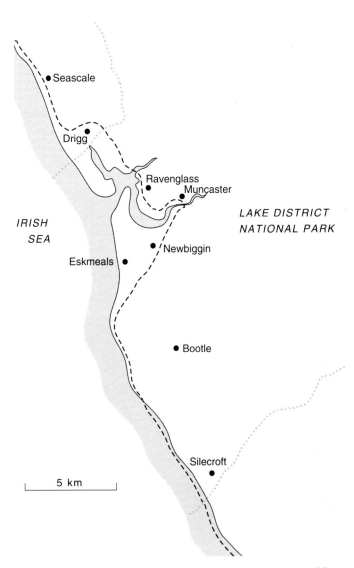

Seascale

Drigg

Ravenglass

Muncaster

IRISH
SEA

LAKE DISTRICT
NATIONAL PARK

Eskmeals

Newbiggin

Bootle

Silecroft

5 km

Just over 1 km (½ mile) south of Silecroft you will have crossed the boundary of Millom Without and Whicham parishes and in so doing you will have entered the Lake District National Park. The sea is no respecter of boundaries and dumps its flotsam and jetsam regardless, although regular clearance efforts are made by National Park staff and volunteers.

Few people associate beaches with the Lake District, yet here we find a fine sandy coastline. The geology and geomorphology add to the interest of this section of the walk. Off the coast, opposite Drigg, at very low tide, you can see the remains of forests, now usually submerged under the sea. Other features of this stretch are the wave-cut glacial clay cliffs of Annaside with their storm beaches below. And where the River Annas joins the sea, longshore drift has created a fine spit. Further north, the triple estuary of the rivers Esk, Mite and Irt makes an unusual setting for the ancient port of Ravenglass.

Selker Bay with the western Lakeland fells beyond.

CHAPTER 7

SILECROFT TO MUNCASTER

Silecroft
The centre of Silecroft village (refreshments available) and the railway station are both about 1.6 km (1 mile) inland from the shore car park. Just inland and on each side of the road lie Shaw Meadow and Sea Pasture, designated an SSSI because of the superb heather and gorse coastal heath with wet habitats, including patches of orchids. Stonechat and white-throat breed here and migrating birds find it an ideal autumn staging post.

Traditional English pastimes are the order of the day at Silecroft – paddling, swimming and lilo riding. In his guide to Cumbria, John Parker suggests other possibilities: 'Beach pebbles are a collector's treasure-house – the varieties of stone include pink and grey granite, black and grey slate, quartz and volcanic tuffs.'

Black Combe
Overshadowing us for much of the way is Black Combe, 600 m (1968 ft), the most south-westerly Lakeland fell. This mat grass moor is composed of Skiddaw Slate, one of Britain's oldest rocks. As well as providing a mariner's landmark, Black Combe served as a guide for early settlers and as the site of a beacon to warn of Scottish forays. It was these raids which gave rise to the saying that 'now't good comes round Black Combe'. If you feel a longing to climb the fell, as a diversion from the Coastal Way, then an ascent from Silecroft, by way of Whicham Church, provides the most direct route.

Wordsworth, in his *Guide to the Lakes*, says of the fell that 'its base covers a much greater extent of ground than any other mountain in those parts; and, from its situation, the summit commands a more extensive view than any other point in Britain.' The view certainly lives up to the poet's praise. We have seen Scotland, the Isle of Man, Wales and into Staffordshire (Jack Hill), and we are told that you can see Ireland.

In recent times beacons have again been lit on the fell, in 1977 for the Silver Jubilee of Queen Elizabeth II and to celebrate the Royal Wedding of 1981.

SILECROFT TO BOOTLE

From Silecroft to Annaside Banks the route lies along a sandy beach below the shingle bank, as on the stretch from Haverigg Point. Thus, to go on the sand, you should time your walk for low tide. Annaside Banks are the final clay cliffs on the walk from Silecroft. A track, at Gutterby Spa, leads up through a break in the cliffs just before this bank.

Birds are in constant flight over the sea. Watch particularly for cormorants near the coast, as well as huge, synchronised flocks of waders. It is not unknown for the odd whale, seal, dolphin or porpoise to be sighted in these waters.

The cliffs we follow to Gutterby and Annaside Banks reach up to 60 m (197 ft) and are composed of compacted mud, stones and boulders (remnants of the ice age). They are very unstable, as the amount of bare earth shows, and with each stormy high tide the sea cuts into them a little more.

Gutterby takes its name from one of its early Norse inhabitants, Godric. The hamlet here once had mineral waters (said to have health-giving properties) flowing from its spring. Between Gutterby and Annaside Banks is a small cove, often with rock pools at low tide, described to Norman Nicholson (in *Greater Lakeland*) as a 'rare place for crabs'.

At Gutterby turn right up the lane, then left immediately before the gate at the top of the slope (or go through the gate and back over the stile to its left). Follow the fence to a

88

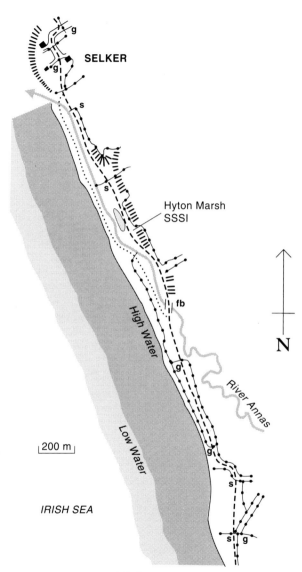

SELKER

Hyton Marsh
SSSI

High Water

Low Water

fb

River Annas

200 m

IRISH SEA

N

Way Map 8: Annaside to Selker

89

stile. Continue, with the sea cliff on your left, to an obvious stile over which an old coach road can be picked up. Follow the old coach road directly ahead by a right-hand fence along the top of Annaside Banks.

On this section of the walk the spectacular Lakeland fells of Pillar, Great Gable and Scafell come into view, as do the cliffs of St Bees Head.

This part of the route is shown on **Way Map 8**. When the track begins to turn inland by the fourth gate, and as farms come into view, cross the stile to the left of the gate. Go down the middle of the field, over another stile, and left down a sunken, gravelly lane to the shore.

Go north along the shore, then into the field on your right, and, going parallel to the shore, and through the gate ahead. Bear right in the next field to cross the bridge over the River Annas. Follow the riverside path, keeping right, by the fence, to pass Hyton Marsh Tarn. Continue towards Selker, taking the diagonal path up the low cliff to a stile. Go over the stile to enter a field near Selker Farm. Head towards the gate on the left-hand side of the farm buildings.

Annaside

The name Annaside is derived from 'Einarr's *saetre*' ('summer pasture') and one can imagine Einarr bringing his flock down from the Black Combe ridge to graze on the saltings in the winter. However life has not always been so peaceful. Apparently the cobblestones from Annaside beach were much sought after in the nineteenth century. Their large-scale removal caused coastal erosion and even led to violence. The *Whitehaven News* gave this stirring account of the Battle of Annaside which took place on the morning of Saturday 18th August in 1838:

> Wilson, a Ravenglass innkeeper, led three boats and a number of Ravenglass inhabitants to load cobbles from the beach at Annaside for Runcorn and Liverpool. The consequences of this

practice was the sea making inroads into the parish and considerable local expenditure to stop it.

With peaceful methods having failed, some three dozen men from Annaside, Bootle and Whitbeck, each carrying a 'good sprig of oak', came to meet Wilson and his male and female followers who had been driven away the day before. Wilson had brought reinforcements and arms [spars and bludgeons] and so incensed the local men to arms.

The paper described the battle:

A most desperate fight ensued, the women pouring in volleys of stones, in addition to the noise they made. In the thick of the fight Wilson signalled himself by a desperate attempt to give a finisher to Mr Parker with the formidable weapon [a huge pump handle], but this circumstance attracted notice, and his sconce was made to crack open again by the repeated blows inflicted upon it by the oaken weapons of his antagonists.

This ended the battle, without the loss of life, but with 'broken heads and bruised bodies'. Some were carried home to be confined to bed 'in a dangerous state' . . . On the turn of the tide the vessels returned to Ravenglass and the language of the women was said to be frightful.

Hyton Marsh SSSI

Where the river bends north to run parallel to the shore before entering the sea is Hyton Marsh SSSI, one of the chain of natterjack toad breeding sites along the Cumbrian Coast. This narrow strip of land between the sea and the river shows the transition from coastal shingle and sand dunes through to dune grassland and semi-improved grassland further inland.

Geographers would call this little piece of land a barrier spit, but why the river flows north when the coastal drift appears to be south is unclear. The River Annas once joined the Irish Sea perhaps 1 km (½ mile) south of its present point but, due to its deltaic load and longshore drift, the mouth has been gradually forced northward.

Follow the access track from Selker Farm as it turns right, to bear inland for Bootle and its railway station. Return to the shore by the gate and follow the edges of the fields, where stiles have been provided. Before you eventually reach the metalled road, where it meets the coast at the public toilets, walk the stretch beside the last two fields below the mean high tide mark. This section of beach is rough under foot and gets flooded at very high tides.

Bootle

Bootle derives its name from Bothill, meaning 'beacon-hill' (no doubt a reference to Black Combe). Formerly part of the great lordship of Millom, Bootle attempted to become a medieval market town and was granted a charter in 1347 for a Wednesday market. Despite this, the village never really succeeded in becoming a prosperous market town. It now sits astride the A595, some 2 km (1¼ miles) from its station.

ESKMEALS TO WABERTHWAITE

Follow the road, with the sea on your left, past the Ministry of Defence Proof and Experimental Establishment (where ammunition is tested) and its main gate. Continue along the road towards the railway until you pass a right-hand turning at an acute angle. Immediately after this, take a track (signed to Eskmeals House) branching off on your right.

If you had continued down the road instead you would have come to Eskmeals viaduct where the railway crosses the estuarine River Esk. The dunes to the west force the Esk north to join the other rivers at Ravenglass.

Drigg Coast SSSI

With the estuary, the dunes form the southern part of the Drigg Coast SSSI. The area has a rich variety of maritime habitats and contains the most extensive sand dune system in Cumbria. It was once the site of a prehistoric settlement and artefacts of the Neolithic and early Bronze Age have been found, including arrowheads, worked flints, and saddle querns for grinding corn.

The Neolithic settlers, who were agriculturalists, came here around 3000 BC. Drigg coast was one of their major sites and they used Walney, Eskmeals and Drigg dunes for their flint workings. (A settlement from this period has also been found at Ehenside Tarn, north of Sellafield.) Some of the tools came from rocks high in the Lakeland fells, such as the Langdale stone axe factory sites. The implements were then polished, using the sandstone rock found on parts of the coast. These people also left stone circles like the one at Swinside.

Drigg Coast SSSI provides good examples of different types of sand dune. The yellow dunes by the sea consist of highly mobile sand. Then, as you come inshore, the dunes start to become more stable, due to colonisation by marram and lyme grasses. In the depressions between the dunes are wet hollows, or slacks, that are rich in flora and provide a home for the natterjack toad.

These dunes were once extensive rabbit warrens. According to the nineteenth-century author, E. Lynn Linton, the rabbits used to cross the estuary by the viaduct to feed around Muncaster. He suggests that before the railway was built they used to swim the Esk!

The Cumbria Wildlife Trust manage Drigg Coast SSSI as a nature reserve. Contact the Trust (see Useful Addresses) before coming to the area.

The old cart ford, just downstream from the viaduct, was regularly used by farm carts until the last war. There are warning notices and depth markers.

The flood tides sometimes cover a few sections of the path between here and Ravenglass. Tide tables and advisory notices are positioned in tidal sections of path near the Esk.

This part of the route is shown on **Way Map 9**. Continue down the drive towards Eskmeals House, passing under the railway bridge. Immediately after the house and a metal gate across a track, look for a kissing gate on your left. Enter the field and aim for the next kissing gate just up from the right-hand field corner. Go through the gate, over the stile facing you, and then cross the nearby footbridge. Go straight ahead into the next field and then bear left near the fence. Go through a further kissing gate by a gate across

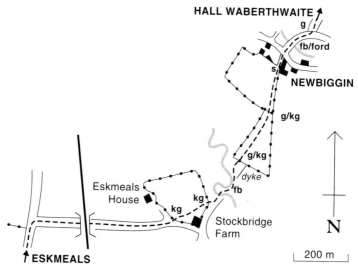

Way Map 9: Eskmeals to Hall Waberthwaite

to the right. Then follow the left-hand hedge, pass through another kissing gate by a gate, and follow the right-hand fence to a stile in the right-hand field corner. Cross this and follow the enclosed path to a further stile. Here you reach the road at Newbiggin.

Go straight across the road and over a footbridge. Beyond the bridge, follow the enclosed track. Go through the second of two adjacent gates, to follow a track branching off to your left. Ignore any side branches, and follow the track through a gate and down to the salt marsh. Continue by the right-hand hedge to emerge, through a gate, by Hall Waberthwaite church.

Waberthwaite

The name Waberthwaite comes from the Norse and means 'the fishing or hunting bothy in the forest clearing'. At Hall Waberthwaite maps show a right of way crossing the tidal Esk by way of a ford. This crossing is said to have originated with the Romans. It was once used on a regular basis by the priest

94

The remote Hall Waberthwaite church.

of Muncaster on his way to preach at the daughter chapel of St John the Evangelist on this bank.

This church is worth a visit in any season, though the graveyard is at its most resplendent at daffodil time. The basic structure is a simple oblong, without chancel or apse and, apart from the fourteenth-century windows and west window stonework, it is still essentially Norman.

Inside, the pews are of the square box variety, and the decor is plain and practical. The font is possibly Norman – a square red sandstone block of early workmanship. The oak pulpit was carved in 1630 and bears a Latin inscription which translates as: 'Woe is me if I preach not the truth'.

The churchyard contains many old tombstones, and at least one burial, in 1678, took place during the wool market glut when bodies had to be wrapped in sheep's wool instead of being placed in a coffin. There is also a cross shaft dating from between the seventh and tenth centuries. It was made by chipping or hacking the local red sandstone, and was refixed into its original socket in 1884 after being temporarily used as

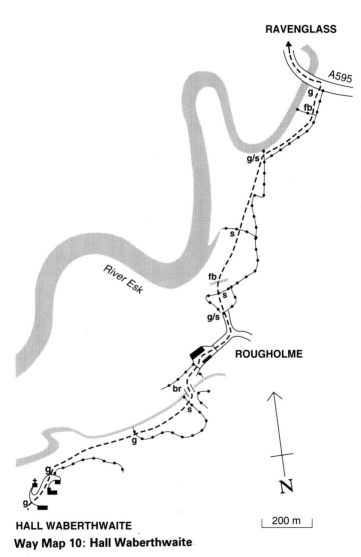

RAVENGLASS

A595

g

fb

g/s

River Esk

s

fb

s

g/s

ROUGHOLME

br

s

g

N

200 m

HALL WABERTHWAITE
Way Map 10: Hall Waberthwaite

a lintel in the porch. Next to it lies a smaller fragment of another cross shaft, possibly tenth century, with foliated vine scroll on the edges. These crosses are remnants of Northumbrian settlers who, after King Eigfrith's conquest of Cumbria in the eighth century, gradually settled around the coast and on the more fertile land between coast and fell.

WABERTHWAITE TO MUNCASTER

This part of the route is shown on **Way Map 10**. Take the track to the right of the church and go down, past the houses, to a gate and into a field. Turn right down the wet track and through the gate in the far left-hand corner. Continue along the track until the right-hand fence bends right. Cross the remaining part of the field to reach the bridge in the left-hand field corner. Over the bridge, climb up to the farmyard, pass through the gated yard of Rougholme and follow the farm access track until it bends sharply right.

Above Waberthwaite are Bootle and Thwaite fells, with cairnfields that date back to Bronze Age times, and the prehistoric settlement of Barnscar which lies below Devoke Water. The pepperpot-style beacon seen above the first line of crags used to help guide shipping into the tricky estuarine harbour at Ravenglass.

Go left down the enclosed track, cross the stile by the gate, drop down through the trees, mostly on a board walk, and cross a further stile. Drop down a short slope and enter the saltings by a small footbridge. Bear right, parallel to the River Esk, and cross the stile halfway along the fence which runs across your path. Go towards the right-hand fence corner of the next field, then continue at the same angle over reedy ground to meet the fence again by a gate and stile next to the river. In the last field follow the right-hand boundary to a footbridge, then go straight ahead to reach the road by a stile adjacent to a gate. Turn left to Muncaster bridge.

CHAPTER 8

MUNCASTER AND RAVENGLASS

MUNCASTER

Continue along the road from the bridge, turn left at Hirst Lodge and follow the track through the wood. Pass through the kissing gate by the field gate, continue along the track through a large field and then through a further kissing gate by a field gate. Continue along the track and note a gate and turnstile on your right leading to Muncaster Castle. This is a section where dogs *must* be kept on a lead.

Muncaster Castle

Here you have an opportunity to visit Muncaster Church, castle and the owl breeding centre in the grounds. Perched on the bluff above the River Esk, with fine views along Eskdale towards the Scafells, Muncaster Castle's romantic situation suits the style of this largely Victorian edifice. If you visit the castle or its grounds pay your dues at the turnstile. The grounds are open most days (except Friday) from 12 a.m. to 5 p.m., and the castle on Tuesday, Wednesday, Thursday and Sunday from 2 p.m. to 5 p.m. between Easter and October. Stick to the public footpath or the official coast path across the grounds if you do not intend to visit.

St Michael's Church was the mother church of Hall Waberthwaite. In many ways it is a typical dale church – its low lines and bellcote reflecting a farming parish very much tied to the castle. However the castle architect, Anthony Salvin, added to the building in 1874 and gave the interior an air of Victorian High Church. Outside in the churchyard there

Muncaster Castle.

is a cross-shaft (possibly eleventh century) displaying a pattern of broad, flat but defaced plaiting.

In the gardens the Terrace Walk is of particular interest and, during rhododendron flowering time, provides a major attraction. You have access to about 14 hectares (35 acres) of gardens and much of the remainder of the 13 000 hectare (32 000 acre) estate has a network of public footpaths. Not too far from the gardens is Muncaster fell which gives extensive views of this part of Lakeland with minimal effort.

The castle was the home of the Penningtons who came to Ravenglass as Lords of the Manor in the twelfth century and may have used Walls Castle, the Roman bath house, as their dwelling until the pele tower (now part of the present castle) was constructed in 1325. Designed as a refuge from Scottish raiders, the tower's walls are 2.5 m (8 ft) thick and it used to contain a spiral staircase.

Architect Anthony Salvin largely rebuilt the castle in 1862–6 but how much of the earlier stonework was retained, apart from the pele tower, is uncertain. The flamboyant architect was kept under tight fiscal control and, perhaps because of this, he used the local red sandstone and pink Esksdale Granite with pleasing results.

In 1461, after his defeat by Yorkists in the battle of Towton, King Henry VI was found wandering in the estate and took shelter in the castle. A tower, seen from the castle, now marks the spot where a shepherd found him. To honour his hosts the King gave them a curious bowl of greenish glass which is still preserved in the castle and is known as the 'Luck of Muncaster'. It is said that the Pennington line will prosper as long as the bowl remains intact.

The King's bedstead and a portrait of him with the 'Luck' can be seen on the castle tour which is conducted by personal stereos collected on entering the house.

From the turnstile continue along the main track through the woods, including Heronry Wood, keeping left at main track junctions to reach the riverside promenade. When opposite the ford to Hall Waberthwaite Church, turn left to pass through a gate and reach the saltings. (This part of the route is shown on **Way Map 11**.) If it is high tide continue a little further along the track and turn right to reach a kissing gate by a gate. This path goes directly up the field and contours round the edge of Newton Knott. It then joins the road through Newton Farm and reaches Ravenglass by way of Walls Castle.

At low tide follow the right-hand side of the saltings and go under the railway arch. Continue straight ahead and then turn right to follow the edge of the estuary into Ravenglass. The ancient salmon garth in the Esk, which is still licensed for use as a salmon fish trap, is passed on the way.

Walls Castle

Walls Castle is actually the remains of a Roman bath house where two former rooms stand almost to full height and still retain some original plaster. It is the tallest Roman building in the north of England. That the damaged arches and overhanging walls still stand is testimony to the Roman knowledge of

Way Map 11: Hall Waberthwaite to Ravenglass

concrete (knowledge that was lost for many centuries). Nikolaus Pevsner describes the ruin thus:

> The actual walls, built of a coursed red freestone and rendered internally with pink mortar, stand to a height of 4 metres. Two doorways survive, each with a shallow relieving arch above the wooden lintel, and there are traces of five splayed windows. The wall of one of the rooms, possibly the entrance hall, contains a round-headed niche, semicircular in plan.

The niche was supposed to hold a sculpture, possibly of a Roman god.

Walls is traditionally linked with the Celts and King Arthur as 'Lyons Garde' or Castle Perilous, the home of King Eveling, or Avalloch, the Celtic Lord of the Underworld. When the Romans came, they absorbed much of the Celtic way of life. Celtic place names and gods were retained and Celtic druids continued to practise their ancient rituals. They used the previously constructed stone circles for their religious festivals, and possibly for keeping track of the passing of time. The druids kept the tribal lore and heritage alive from generation to generation. They were the spiritual leaders of the people who lived in this part of Britain. There were also druids in Ireland and the Isle of Man, and the Irish Sea would have been their major channel of communication.

When the Romans arrived local tribes, such as the Cumbrae (who were part of the Brigantes nation), seem to have been a thorn in their flesh. These tribes did not accept colonisation easily. Hadrian's Wall may have been built to keep the English Brigantes away from the Celtic tribes north of the wall, as well as vice versa.

The bath house is near the site of a Roman fort but this was damaged by the construction of the railway and the planting of conifers. Some historians have argued that this was the southernmost fort of the Solway defence system leading to Hadrian's Wall, whilst others, because of its inward facing defences, say that it couldn't have been part of that system.

RAVENGLASS

Ravenglass is one of the places along the route where it's worth setting aside some time to explore. It is well supplied with shops and eating places and, although the port has long since silted over, there is still much of interest to be seen.

It was perhaps during the Roman occupation that Ravenglass had its most important role, though followers of Celtic history may disagree. The port of Glannaventa, where three estuaries disgorge into the Irish Sea, was established to provide a supply base for inland forts, northern defences and possible conquests of western Scotland or Ireland, as well as a place of commerce. Some writers believe this was Agricola's main port and quote records of trade with the major Roman garrison of Chester.

Since those glamorous times, the port has had other colourful eras. Writing in the early years of this century, A. G. Bradley commented:

> No doubt, every soul inhabiting the double row of queer old-fashioned tenements is usefully and worthily employed, in some way or other, but not, I take it, after the manner of their predecessors, for smuggling is writ large all over Ravenglass, and it has a delightfully wicked appearance, though it does nothing, I believe, more reckless nowadays than gather mussels.

The smuggling involved both the import of contraband goods and the export of illicitly distilled whisky by the Honister quarrymen. This was transported at night to the port on pack ponies with sacking over their hooves. Stolen wadd or plumbago (graphite) from the mine in Borrowdale is another local material that may have taken the smugglers' export route.

The port was active until the middle of the eighteenth century and some cargo vessels even called here last century. Much of their business would have been linked with the annual fair of St James the Apostle. Permission to hold this three-day fair was granted by King John in 1208 during a sojourn at Kendal Castle when he also gave Richard de Lucy, Lord of Egremont, the right to hold a Saturday market in the township. Boats would bring cattle over from Ireland, the Isle of Man and Scotland for the fair. Sail-powered coasters served the area into the early years of this century.

Graham Sutton, a Cumbrian novelist who went to school at St Bees, has written five books that tell the story of a local family of sheep farmers through the centuries and these have frequent references to the Cumbrian Coast, particularly between Ravenglass and Workington. The books are entitled *Shepherd's Warning*, *Smoke Across the Fell*, *North Star*, *Fleming of Honister* and the last written, but chronologically earlier to the others, *The Rowan Tree*. Sutton knew the area and its history very well and this gives the novels added realism. Some of Hugh Walpole's *Herries Chronicles* also have references to this section of the coast. With their vivid writing and strong storylines, it's strange that the sagas of Walpole and Sutton have not yet made it on to our television screens.

The three rivers that join the sea at Ravenglass carry a great deal of Lakeland's rainfall, for they drain the valleys of Eskdale, Mitredale and Wasdale.

La'al Ratty

The major tourist attraction in the area is the Ravenglass and Eskdale Narrow Gauge Railway. It is more affectionately known as 'La'al Ratty', supposedly after Mr Ratcliffe, the building contractor for the Whitehaven Mining Company who operated the Boot, Eskdale, haematite mines. The first ore train on the 3-foot gauge railway ran on 24th May 1875, and soon after began to carry passengers.

The mines ceased operating in 1912 and in 1915 the line was acquired as a public railway. A narrower 15-inch track was laid and started being used to transport Eskdale granite. Today the narrow gauge steam and diesel trains operate a regular passenger service from Ravenglass, up by the Mite and then over into Eskdale. The views are excellent and it's a good ramble back from Eskdale Green station, over Muncaster Fell, to Ravenglass.

The Ravenglass and Eskdale Railway, or 'La'al Ratty'.

There is a preserved corn mill near the railway terminus in Boot and also a working watermill by the railway just outside Ravenglass. Both are open from Easter to September, every day except Saturday, from 11 a.m. to 5 p.m.

105

CHAPTER 9

RAVENGLASS
TO SEASCALE

RAVENGLASS TO DRIGG

From the inland end of Main Street, Ravenglass, cross the River Mite by the footbridge on the railway viaduct. It is possible to use the ford at low tide but it can be muddy. Continue along the shoreside track, pass through Saltcoates and bear right at the junction of the metalled roads. Please note that at very high tides the path to the farm can be flooded.

Continue on the road, cross the railway by the level crossing, and continue until you reach Mite Houses on your right. Turn left off the metalled road down a straight, enclosed, pleasant green lane. At the end of the lane turn right on the metalled road. When this road bends right leave by the track on the left. Follow this enclosed track, bending right by the field gates on each side, and over the stile in the fence across your way. Go directly over the interconnecting field track and follow the remainder of the lane to a further stile in the field corner that gives you access to a field. (See **Way Map 12** for the route from this area to Drigg.)

Cross this field, passing an overhead wire pole, and, looking down to the river, enter the wood ahead by a stile. Follow the right-hand hedge, then go down some steep steps and cross the River Irt by the attractively humped Holme Bridge.

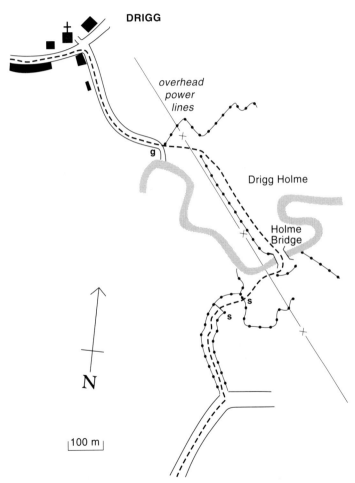

Way Map 12: Drigg Holme.

DRIGG

overhead
power
lines

g

Drigg Holme

Holme
Bridge

s

s

N

100 m

The River Irt

After draining England's deepest lake and highest fell, the River Irt appears a somewhat tame stream unless it is in flood. Some of its water is extracted for use at Sellafield.

Like other clear, fast mountain rivers with a low lime content the Irt harbours the mussel *Margaritifera margaritifera*. These black river mussels were once fished for here on account of their pearls. It is thought that the locals sold the pearls to the Romans. However this trade is better documented in later times.

Sir John Hawkins, a sixteenth-century circumnavigator, held the patent for pearl fishing in the river. In 1777 it is recorded that London pearl dealers paid £800 to local fishermen for pearls. Even the famous Elizabethan historian Camden uses the phrase 'fair as Irton pearls'.

Most of the pearl beds were exhausted during the eighteenth century but small seed pearls were still being collected hereabouts during World War II. The pearlers used glass-bottomed drums when searching for the host mussels and even these days some Scottish pearlers intermittently search the river using this traditional method. The River Ehen, crossed later, also had a pearl fishery.

Nearby are Carleton Hall, a late Georgian House, and Holmrook Hall, which was noted for its gardens and rare trees. Crossing Holme Bridge takes us out of the National Park.

Over the bridge, go up the field (called Drigg Holme), staying parallel to the overhead wires and the left-hand hedge, with views to Wasdale. When the hedge bends left continue towards the pylon ahead and pick up a track. Follow this track left to the field corner to meet an enclosed track that leads into Drigg. Turn left on the road at the end of the track.

Drigg

Drigg Holme is the former common field where the tenant farmers used the run-rig system. This ensured that every farmer had in his holding each year a fair share of each soil type. In this area the soil consists chiefly of sand with varying mixtures of loam. The local seaweed, refered to as 'tangle', would no doubt have been used as a source of green manure, a practice that was common along the coast. The field is now an SSSI.

St Peter's Church, Drigg, was built in 1850 of the local red sandstone. It is a simple but solid dale chapel. On a tomb in the churchyard will be found this appropriate comment:

Spectators all as you pass by,
As, you are now, so once was I,
But, as I am, so you must be,
Prepare for Death and follow me.

Shipwrecks were not uncommon on this coast in earlier times and the locals, even the church goers, were often more interested in looting the vessels than helping the survivors. It is said that a parson of Drigg who was conducting a service one stormy Sunday left instructions that the west door of the church be left open so that he might see when the vessel in distress off the coast was washed ashore. His parishioners were also keenly interested but they had two advantages over the parson – they were not encumbered with surplices and they were nearer the door. When the ship struck land there was a general rush from the congregation as the parson implored: 'Nay, nay, lads; let us have fair play.'

Drigg Hall, near the church, is late Georgian and, unusually for this neck of the woods, partially constructed of brick.

After joining the road through the village turn left at the junction, go past the station and down the shore road. Follow the road down to the coast.

The Victoria Hotel and a craft shop will be found at the station. On the way down, the road sweeps round an area of trees planted in an attempt to disguise the site of a wartime explosives factory, now a low-level radioactive materials dump owned by British Nuclear Fuels. Contaminated equipment and clothing, for example, will be buried in trenches on this site which will be left landscaped when it is full.

Drigg Dunes

Drigg Dunes lie south of here and stretch right back to the estuary at Ravenglass, forming a major portion of the Drigg Coast SSSI. A track goes down to the Ravenglass Local Nature Reserve, established in 1954 and now managed by the Lake District National Park Authority.

Local people once collected the eggs of nesting black-headed gulls from this area but when they arrived at London hotels they had mysteriously turned into plover eggs.

The reserve's main feature is its dune habitats, where the largest English population of black-headed gulls, along with terns, tiger and dung beetles, natterjack toads and adders are all to be found. Flora recorded includes Carline thistle, marsh felwort, bloody cranesbill, yellow-horned poppy and Portland spurge on the dunes, whilst the saltings hold glasswort, sea purslane and sea lavender. On the shingle the Isle of Man cabbage and cinnabar moth caterpillars can be found on the ragwort. Other butterflies and moths include the small copper, meadow brown, small tortoiseshell and peacock.

Off shore are the remains of a considerable deposit of peat and the submarine remnants of a forest. These can be seen at very low tides and blocks of peat may be washed up along the shore.

Neolithic arrowheads and Beaker folk burial sites been discovered on this section of the coast and, around 1670, Sir William Pennington of Muncaster established a course for horse races on the sands.

The large boulder just off the coast is called Carl Crag. It is said to have been dropped by the Devil in an unsuccessful attempt to build a bridge to the Isle of Man. (This is the point where the Isle of Man is nearest to England.)

O.S. maps mark this part of the coast with red danger areas. This is because the currents sometimes wash up shells that didn't explode at Eskmeals testing site. Please don't try to succeed where the Ministry of Defence have failed.

DRIGG TO SEASCALE

Turn right, along the shoreline, with floral interest amongst the dunes on your right, until you arrive in Seascale. This section is best walked after the tide has ebbed. A short path across the dunes, starting from behind the ruined hut, will help you avoid the first section of the beach if the tide is still in.

Seascale

Seascale, which means 'the hut by the sea', marks the end of this section. Baddeley, the doyen of Victorian Lake District guide book writers, describes this small seaside town and sandy beach as 'the best headquarters on the west coast'. The giant complex of Sellafield didn't overshadow the town in those days.

Seascale was another town planned by Sir James Ramsden for the Furness Railway. It was to be a second Eastbourne, a setting for the Victorian family seaside holiday that was the fashion of the day. However the demand was not there and only a small fraction of the development, to the north of the station, was completed.

Architecturally, Nikolaus Pevsner wasn't taken with the place, saying only, 'On the sea front there is nothing to report'. But he can't have noticed Herding Nab Cottage on the shore road, with a figurehead over its porch that came from a vessel stormwrecked in January 1884. The cottage was originally an inn and was patronised by local poachers until the Lord of the Manor prevented the renewal of the licence. They assumed it was because 'they wadna leav him a hare aboot t'spot'.

Just north of Seascale lies Grey Croft with its reconstructed stone circle about 25 m (82 ft) in diameter. A farmer buried the original twelve stones in the nineteeth century, and the circle now consists of ten stones which were dug up and reinstated in 1949.

SECTION FOUR
THE
WEST CUMBRIAN
COAST

Maryport

Flimby

Workington

Harrington

Parton

Whitehaven

5 km

St Bees

Nethertown

IRISH
SEA

Sellafield

Seascale

113

Section Four: The West Cumbrian Coast

The West Cumbrian coast is a place where men and women and children have always toiled to exploit the riches of the earth. Because jobs have often been hard to come by, work is the main priority here – sometimes at great cost to the environment.

Both the Lake District and the Cumbrian coast have a long industrial history, based on their abundant natural resources and helped to reach a wider market by the advent of railways and, more recently road communications.

Following the Norman colonisation of the county, with the early exploitation of resources such as water power, woodlands (including charcoal manufacture), iron ore, minerals and coal, industrial development continued through the Middle Ages under the auspices of wealthy monasteries.

Later on, in the seventeenth and eighteenth centuries, local landed families played their part in developing the area. But it was the Victorian industrial revolution which had the most lasting impact. In this era coal, iron ore and transport became increasingly important in the economy of Cumbria, and it is these industries which have largely shaped the landscape on the West Cumbrian coast, leaving a valuable industrial heritage legacy which is disappearing all too quickly.

Apart from this industrial inheritance there are scenic delights and wildlife to see on this stretch. The three major towns and their people add to the character of the walk. Most West Cumbrians are welcoming and friendly and you will find it difficult to pass local people without an exchange of greetings. Yes, you can get on the train and pass by in minutes what deserves a few days of your time, but you will be the poorer for it. In this section some industrial complexes welcome visitors and your appreciation of wild landscape will be heightened when you realise that an industrial landscape is but another facet of our man-made countryside. The fact is that there is no countryside left in England that is really untouched by human influence.

Inland from St Bees and Whitehaven can be seen the rugged central Lakeland fells, including England's highest peak Scafell Pike. These towering fells were produced by under-sea volcanoes which spewed out their lavas and ash to form the rocks we now call the Borrowdale Volcanic Group. After the spell of deposition of Carboniferous Limestone a huge upheaval forced the rocks of Lakeland into a central dome. In the warm, arid desert conditions that followed, the limestone capping was removed and sands were deposited in surrounding basins. These sediments consolidated to form the St Bees Sandstone. This red-coloured rock, often used in buildings from Millom to Maryport, is best seen in the dramatic cliffs at St Bees Head.

CHAPTER 10

SEASCALE TO ST BEES

SEASCALE TO SELLAFIELD

From Seascale station follow the path on the shoreward side of the railway until the River Calder enters the sea. Go under the railway bridge, cross the Calder by the British Nuclear Fuels (BNFL) bridge and continue alongside the railway to Sellafield station.

Calder Hall, Windscale, Sellafield . . .

The River Ehen, from Ennerdale, joins the River Calder only a few metres short of where they plunge together over the shingle beach into the Irish Sea. Longshore drift, south from St Bees Head, has moved the river mouth south of its original position and created a spit.

During the war the Sellafield site was a munitions factory. Since then it has had the eyes of the world focused on it. Here, in 1956, the Queen opened the world's first commercial nuclear reactor, Calder Hall. With a maximum output of 600 megawatts, this graphite-moderated, gas-cooled reactor held some 130 tonnes of natural uranium fuel.

Calder Hall should be generating current until 2000 AD but is due to be replaced by a gas turbine station to supply the site's power. For the longer term, BNFL are investigating the feasibility of constructing a large pressurised water reactor to the north of the site.

The dome-shaped building on the Windscale site is the pioneer advanced gas-cooled reactor which was commissioned in February 1963. It served as a research reactor, whilst

The restored Grey Croft Stone Circle, with Sellafield beyond.

delivering some 3.7 billion kilowatt hours of electricity to the National Grid, before it was switched off in April 1981. This site will be decommissioned.

North of the river lies Sellafield, formerly Windscale, the site of Britain's nuclear fuel reprocessing facility. Here plutonium is also extracted, giving rise to claims that Sellafield is the source of radioactive discharges into the Irish Sea and into the atmosphere. Here lies the controversial THORP plant and the possible site of an underground nuclear repository. There is a free exhibition in the visitors' centre and conducted coach tours around the massive site. It is curious how the PR men use names: originally Sellafield, then Windscale, then Calder Works, and now . . . Sellafield.

The infamous Windscale piles, a crude nuclear power plant that was used primarily to generate plutonium for the country's atomic bomb, has been closed following a nuclear accident in 1957, and is now being dismantled.

The railway station is called Sellafield and this is the place Baddeley, author of a late nineteenth-century guide to the Lake District, could find no local accommodation at all. In the days when such stations were manned a porter once entertained waiting passengers with accounts of his hobby – astronomy. Another surprising Sellafield fact: according to some meteorological records it is the sunniest place in Cumbria.

SELLAFIELD TO ST BEES

> Pass the entrance to the station, continue alongside the railway and when you reach two gates facing the end of the road pass through the left-hand one. Walk forward, go under the pipe bridge, and turn right to climb the hill. Follow the hilltop fence on your right. Continue over stiles, downhill along an enclosed path and left down some steps. Then, via further stiles, cross the field and the railway bridge over the River Ehen where sandmartins nest and the goosander and heron feed.
>
> On the far bank, go down under the railway arch, then turn right to walk along the flower-speckled raised beach. Continue near the railway line and then by the edge of the beach, using the track that links the chalets.

This stretch is best walked at low tide. To the west, you can see the Isle of Man. Look out for semi-precious stones and bird life on the quieter sections. The next few miles can often be quite tough underfoot.

Some of the chalets look rather neglected but many are much loved. They may be an eyesore but so is the massive caravan site just beyond the railway. For their owners they are heaven, a breathing space from industry.

> A series of beach chalets begins just short of Braystones station. Continue past the station and along until you see a bridge over the railway.

A little way inland from Braystones was Ehenside Tarn. When it was drained in the 1870s interesting examples of Neolithic pottery, stone axes and wooden implements were found. The settlement would have been in a marshy area and may have remained occupied into Roman times.

Nethertown

> You can continue along the beach to pass Nethertown but the alternative route – through the village and back to the seaward side of the railway by the station – is recommended

118

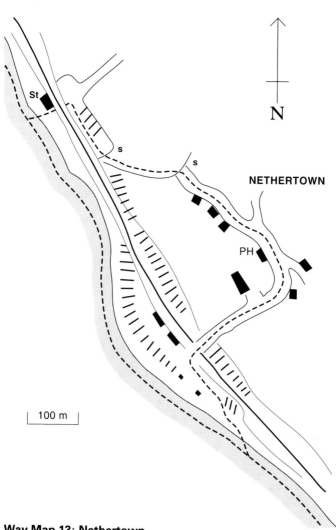

N

St

s

s

NETHERTOWN

PH

100 m

Way Map 13: Nethertown

if you need lunchtime refreshment (see **Way Map 13**). Go to the track that climbs past the chalets and goes across the prominent bridge over the railway. Continue along this track into Nethertown where, besides the caravan sites, you will find a pub, The Tourists, and the village country club and fitness centre.

Turn left, past the pub, and when the road bears right go left down a lane signed to Nethertown station. Pass the last bungalow, continue round the bend, then cross the stile at the end and a further stile facing it. Turn left to follow the fence where another stile gives you a view back down to the coast. Descend to the station and go to the far end of the platform. Turn right to follow the track under the railway and onto the shore. Turn right along the shore.

The direct route continues round the eroded boulder clay headland. After the last beach chalet and the exposed sandstone base rocks you come to the first chalet at St Bees – immediately after the railway has turned inland. You can continue to follow the shore to the Seacote Hotel – the Way goes along the top of the clay cliffs by the edge of the golf course and down to the rear of the hotel which you pass on its left-hand side.

ST BEES

Alternatively you may want to go into St Bees (see **Way Map 14**). After the first chalets, cross the stream and the stile to your right (before the golf course). Go down the field until you see a footbridge on your right over the beck. Cross the beck and continue up the banking, over the railway and up to Sea Mill Lane. Turn left down Main Street to St Bees station, school and refreshments.

You will notice that along this stretch the railway has become single tracked and the elements are waging a constant battle against the crumbling boulder clay cliffs along which it runs. High tides and storms batter the track and the tipping of limestone and concrete, sandstone and slag will only temporarily delay the day when further work has to be done. We

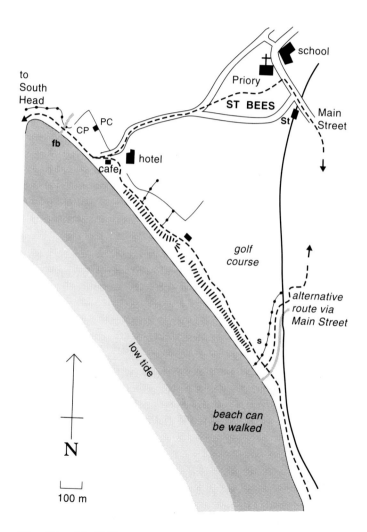

to South Head

PC

CP

fb

cafe

hotel

Priory

ST BEES

school

St

Main Street

golf course

alternative route via Main Street

s

low tide

beach can be walked

N

100 m

Way Map 14: St Bees

121

hope any such work will be carried out with more concern for our adjacent Way.

As the huge car park and caravan site indicate, St Bees is a popular summer holiday resort. Here starts Wainwright's Coast to Coast Walk, a route we will share for the next 6 km (4 miles).

The greater part of the settlement is situated away from the sea, in the lea of the coastal drumlins and near Pow Beck. There are some attractive older houses above the railway station, including some early Elizabethan examples (such as 19–20 Finkle Street). They are made of St Bees Sandstone, a much sought after building stone of gritty texture once used for polishing and sharpening Neolithic stone axes.

The name St Bees is derived from that of an Irish saint, Bega, who was supposed to have founded a nunnery here in 650 AD. There is little evidence to support this story but it is still an interesting legend.

According to tradition, Bega was an Irish princess who fled her homeland to escape an unwanted marriage with a heathen Viking. She came ashore at the site where St Bees now stands (the point where England is nearest to Ireland). This relatively sheltered bay, marked by St Bees Head to the north (which can be seen from the Isle of Man), was a major Viking landing area in Cumbria.

Bega reputedly asked the local landowner, the Lord of Egremont, for lands to form her nunnery. His Lordship, with splendid Christian charity, offered her all the lands covered by snow on midsummer's day (St John's Day in June). There was a fairly extensive snowfall that year. However the nunnery was later apparently destroyed by the Vikings.

St Bees Church

Whatever the truth of the matter it is known that a Benedictine priory, dedicated to St Bega, was founded here in about 1120 by William de Meschines, a Norman Baron of Copeland. Parts of the building have been dated to around 1150.

The priory prospered, acquiring lands in the Lake District dales, interests in the local iron-ore mines, salt-pans and stone quarries (including one that provided stone for St George's Chapel, Windsor), and land around Whitehaven and in the Isle of Man. Small bell pits are sometimes accidentally discovered in the area and these are attributed to this period.

St Bega's Priory, a daughter cell of St Mary's Abbey of York, grew to be the richest in Cumberland but Scottish raids, coupled with local conflicts and rivalries, prevented it from reaching its full economic potential. A fire started by troopers in 1315 caused serious damage and Henry VIII finally dissolved the house in 1539.

From 1539 it became an ordinary church and in 1611 it was reconstructed as the parish church of St Mary and St Bega. Today it still retains some of its Norman stonework, the finest part being the west doorway (dated about 1150).

Nikolaus Pevsner described the church doorway as 'the richest in the county, of three orders of columns, with scrolly capitals including figure-work and much zig-zag and also some sparse beakhead inside the arch'. The beakheads are of men and serpents, and carved on one of the capitals is a figure swinging like a monkey.

The lintel opposite the west door, showing St Michael fighting the dragon among curious early knots and frets, is said to have come from a chapel of St Michael once situated at nearby Rottingham.

The interior is lofty and spacious with a modern nave roof above the arcade of six bays. A windowless wall carved with tracery shuts off most of the chancel. The plain windows in the south transept are also Norman, as is the crossing.

The crossing tower has been restored in the English style, and the nave has some similar work. The screen was made of wrought iron in 1886. A more modern and touching monument is to a child of four. The little figure lies asleep on a tomb under a recess, with a spray of lilies in her hand.

Outside in the churchyard there are two fragmentary cross-shafts, one with interlace, the other with untidy spirals and scrols. Some of the tombstones are over 800 years old, and are carved with crosses, swords and shears. A particularly fine one shows an archer drawing his bow.

The priory originally occupied the land which is now wooded between the church and school library. In 1981, archaeologists discovered, on the site of a ruined priory chapel, one of the best-preserved medieval bodies in England. After examination they identified the body as a local lord who lived in the fourteenth century. The remains were then reburied. Further information, hair and a burial shroud can be seen in the Whitehaven Museum.

St Bees School

Behind the priory lies St Bees School, founded in 1583 by Edmund Grindal of Hensingham, a man Elizabeth I was to make Archbishop of York and later Canterbury. His coat of arms is carved in stone over the main entrance to the school. Born in the village of St Bees in 1517, Grindal's house still stands on the corner of Finkle Street and Cross Hill.

The centre of the school lies opposite the chancel, and the north wing is the original schoolhouse. The builders possibly recycled stone from the priory. The south wing was built in the 1840s and the chapel and headmaster's house early this century.

St Bees School, built from the local sandstone.

CHAPTER 11

ST BEES
TO WHITEHAVEN

This next stretch of the Way lies over the twin north and south St Bees Heads, an area designated as a Heritage Coast. From here to Whitehaven the Way mostly traverses land owned by Albright and Wilson (a large manufacturer of chemical products). It is largely through this company's close collaboration, and particularly that of their former PR man, Mike Clay, with the British Trust for Conservation Volunteers that this section became the first part of the Way to be officially opened. The co-operation of Copeland Borough Council and the Royal Society for the Protection of Birds were also key factors.

ST BEES HEADS

The twin Heads of Baruth (*Barr-ruadh* being the Irish for 'red-head') rise to 100 m (305 ft), the highest coastal point in the north-west of England and the highest altitude reached on the Way.

The red sandstone that forms these cliffs (called the St Bees Sandstone) was laid down in desert conditions some 240 million years ago. The cliffs now mark the point where beach material from the North Head is carried north towards the Solway. From the South Head the direction of drift is south towards Walney.

It is possible that the headland marked the end of the chain of Roman signal stations that stretch northwards along the coast to Hadrian's Wall. The headland forms the southern boundary of the Solway and also served as a beacon site, linking with St Michael's Mount, Workington, and Newton Knott, Muncaster, to warn of Scottish raids.

South Head

From the seafront car park go towards the South Head and climb the distinct path up, over and down to Fleswick Bay. To cross this small valley and stream, the Way skirts round above the defile, via two stiles. However a diversion to the bay at low tide will be amply rewarded.

The South Head or Tomlin is the least interesting of the two but some old walling and coastal plants are to be seen – including thirft, sea campion and sea plantain – particularly on the cliff ledges. Where wet 'seeps' are present then golden saxifrage and watercress can be spotted. Nonetheless the cliff is a superb viewpoint, both southwards towards Black Combe and towards the North Head.

Below the South Head lies a site, mostly eroded by the sea, where Mesolithic stone blades and small flints for tools were produced.

Fleswick Bay was once the haunt of smugglers and it is easy to imagine the small dark caves holding kegs of brandy and bottles of whisky which, according to William Palmer, were 'overproof and innocent of excise formalities'.

The bay is a good place for semi-precious stones such as agates and has a wonderfully sculpted sandstone shore.

North Head

Continue along the path by the fence that climbs and follows the edge of North Head. Pass between the light-house and coastguard's lookout and follow the path to arrive at Birkam's Quarry and cottage. (This is where the Coast to Coast walk leaves the Coastal Way.) There are several stiles along the route and one or two exposed pieces of path. A right-hand fence accompanies you almost all the way but in two places the path climbs into the field on the right where you follow the left-hand fence.

The North Head has the major attraction of an RSPB reserve. Already by 1974 the site had been declared an SSSI, due to its ornithological, topographical and botanical interest. The cliffs form one of England's major seabird nesting sites, with populations of herring gull, kittiwake, guillemot and razorbill running into many thousands of pairs. The clifftop vegetation also provides nesting opportunities for other species. This is the only English nesting site, albeit for a handful, of black guillemot. Chough once nested here and peregrine falcon, stonechat, shag, puffin, kestrel, little owl, rock pipit, grey wagtail, wren, whitethroat, willow warbler, raven and, in more recent times, fulmer have been recorded.

Besides birds, rabbits, slow worms and fifteen species of butterfly can to be found. As for flora, the clifftop grasslands harbour sea pinks, scurvy grass, cocksfoot grass and York-shire fog, besides more common species including bloody cranesbill, wood vetch, bitter vetch, orpine, knapweed and yarrow. On the drier banks are harebell, yellow hawkweed, tormentil and thyme.

During the reign of Charles II, and perhaps in more recent times of hardship, birds have been netted from the headland for food.

The earliest lighthouse on North Head was built in 1718 to replace an earlier beacon. A second, coal-burning light was destroyed by fire in 1822 and the current structure was erected in 1866–7. A white, fixed light gives two flashes every twenty seconds from the 17 m (56 ft) high tower to guide boats into Whitehaven. The light can be seen from the Isle of Man, here almost at its nearest point to England.

As well as Nicholson, St Bees Heads have moved other literary figures. Thomas Carlyle, remembering them from his native Dumfriesshire across the Solway, described them as that 'sappyre promontory'. Wordsworth perambulated around them and also sailed past them on his way to the Isle of Man. In the 'Poems Composed or Suggested During a Tour, in the Summer of 1833' there is a collection of 'Stanzas Suggested in a Steamboat Off Saint Bees' Head, on the Coast of Cumberland':

Dread cliffs of Baruth! that wild wish may sleep,
Bold as if men and creatures of the Deep
Breathed the same element; too many wrecks
Have struck thy sides, too many ghastly decks
Hast thou looked down upon, that such a thought
Should here be welcome, and in verse enwrought:
With thy stern aspect better far agrees
Utterance of thanks that we have past with ease,
As millions thus shall do, the Headlands of St Bees.

ST BEES HEADS TO WHITEHAVEN

When the Coast to Coast walk goes right at Birkam's continue ahead beneath the once quarried cliffs with Whitehaven now in sight. Continue on the path, pass the plaque commemorating the opening of the first section, and continue until the left-hand tip abuts the track. Turn left and follow the path across and down the far side of the graded tip and go down to the right-hand side of the wire netting above the discharge pipe. Beyond, follow a path along the cliff-edge fields (with a fence mostly to the right but on two occasions going into the field) to a track. Keep left to pass below the buildings and pithead wheel at the former Haig Pit until you reach a track and a signpost pointing left and down to Saltom Pit.

Albright and Wilson

Albright and Wilson's Marchon works began as a company making firelighters from local supplies of sawdust, naphthalene and coal-tar residues and is now the largest sulphuric acid-making plant in Britain. The plant produces toiletries such as shampoos and soapless detergents which form the basis of industrial and domestic washing powders and cleaning agents.

Raw materials have to be brought to the plant. Liquid sulphur, from Texas, and phosphoric acid are imported into Workington. Sodium carbonate or sodium hydroxide, to neutralise the acids produced, once came by rail and used to arrive directly at the hilltop factory by a steep and impressive

Albright and Wilson's Marchon Factory near Whitehaven.

incline railway. Alas they are now transported from the sidings below by road. At the plant, surfactants (foaming products) are made from vegetable sources such as palm kernel oil for shampoos and bubble baths, and from mineral oil derivatives for detergent liquids and powders.

It seems a little odd to choose a hilltop site for a plant that needs so many raw materials but the original, and maybe future, raw materials for manufacturing sulphuric acid were anhydrite and gypsum (calcium sulphate), found in plentiful supply beneath the St Bees Sandstone of the North Head and adjacent areas.

In view of Whitehaven's important links with the British chemical industry, it is rather apt that this town was once the home of Dr Brownrigg, an eighteenth-century physician and chemist. He gave the first detailed account of platinum, a metal which had arrived at Whitehaven port from the West Indies in 1741, and was also the first to realise that air contained carbon dioxide and was therefore acidic.

Coal

The export of coal is the major reason for the existence of Whitehaven and similar towns along this stretch of coast, for between St Bees Head and Maryport lies the seaward edge of the West Cumberland coalfield of Middle Coal Measures. These heavily faulted strata of Carboniferous rocks dip deep beneath the Irish Sea. The coal is of the bituminous class best used for steam raising, coking and household fuel. British Coal have now closed all their mines and are winding down their open-cast operations in Cumbria, although one or two small private drift mines still work in the area intermittently.

The coalfield of West Cumbria first apppears to have been systematically worked in about 1620 by Sir Christopher Lowther at Whitehaven, on estates previously owned by St Bees Priory. His son, Sir John, put a great deal of money into driving levels, introducing winding engines and developing the economic base of the coalfield. The family continued to develop the field and in 1718 Sir James Lowther set up their first steam engine for pumping water from the pits. The Lowthers managed the entire coalfield until 1888 when they let one of the mines to Whitehaven Colliery Company.

In its earlier days the West Cumbrian coalfield was at the forefront of technological developments, especially due to the work of the Lowthers' local mining and land agents, the Speddings, who were responsible for pioneering work on deep pumping and utilising gas for lighting.

Prior to mechanisation, horses were used underground. Galloways, with panniers, originally took the coal to the quayside and brought the empty wagons back. They were also used to lift coal from the pits and to operate 'ginns' to drain the pits. Thus there was an important parallel horse industry. Whilst the horses themselves were not expensive, and even the worn-out horses were sold if they had not died, their food was not cheap.

Haig Pit

This last stretch of the Way into Whitehaven goes over the reclaimed site of Haig Pit which was originally sunk around

1916 by the Whitehaven Colliery Company. This company folded in 1933 but not until it had suffered four mining disasters, resulting in the loss of 83 lives.

Haig was worked together with the nearby shafts of Thwaite (originally sunk in 1737) and Wellington Pit (sunk in 1840). During the mid-thirties Haig Colliery lay idle until it was reopened in March 1937, after improvements to the shafts and airways. In 1939 they installed an underground train which operated until the pit closed. It carried 140 men on each of two trains to the face and was worked on an endless rope haulage system.

By the time it closed in the 1980s there were six parallel roadways going due west under the Solway for 5 km (3 miles) and the workings went a further 2 km (1¼ miles) westwards. Latterly the coal was delivered by conveyor belt to a system of tubs that brought it to the surface. Four seams, varying from 1 to 4 m (3 to 13 ft) thick, were mined. Between the seams lay bands of fireclay.

Before it closed, over 1000 men were employed to produce around 15 500 tonnes of coal per week. In the main, the coal went to the Moss Bay steelworks, or was sold for local domestic use and for shipment to Ireland.

Saltom Pit
Saltom Bay, like other coastal sites with the name 'salt' was once a site where precious salt was extracted from seawater using salt-pans. The bay is allegedly another smugglers' cove.

Saltom Pit, sunk in 1731, was the first under-sea colliery in the country and remained in operation until 1848. The pithead complex stood on a rock platform about 7 m (23 ft) above sea level between Saltom Bay cliffs and the shore. A scheme to conserve the main engine and winding house was begun in 1991.

The eighteenth-century technological genius Carlisle Spedding solved the problem of inflammable methane at a shaft depth of over 80 m (262 ft) by piping it to the top and offering it for sale for the illumination of Whitehaven! Then, as a result of extensive experimentation, he invented a 'steel

131

mill' to provide underground lighting that would not ignite methane in the pits. There is an article about the construction of the pit in the 1991 Transactions of the Cumberland and Westmorland Archaeological Society.

The usual method of natural ventilation, through parallel shafts, was not possible at Saltom. Its elliptical-shaped shaft (still there under a concrete slab) was therefore partitioned to enable fresh air to replace the 'damp' air containing the inflammable methane.

Another innovation of Spedding's at this pit was a large Newcombe atmospheric engine to drain the seam which slopes steeply under the sea. However horses were still needed to turn rotating drums which raised the coal, in stages, from the pit and up the cliff. From here it went down the wagonway to the Whitehaven coal staithes where the coal was loaded on to the ships.

There was once a much wider track from Harbour View in Whitehaven to this area, on which local people would promenade. During the 1926 pit strike, miners even set up a dance floor by the track for use on summer evenings. The reclaimed tips along this stretch of the coast provide a habitat for 'opportunist' plants which thrive on newly disturbed ground. Species include coltsfoot, daisy, scurvy grass, hawk-weed, ribwort plantain, white clover and scentless mayweed.

Into Whitehaven

Continue along the path above the edge of the cliff, pick up a track and follow it until you eventually come in sight of Wellington Pit chimney. Go down past the chimney, and left in front of the old gatehouse. Follow the path left down to South Beach and then alongside Whitehaven Harbour. Continue round the quays until bollards cross your path. Turn right into Duke Street, and left down Tangier Street, to arrive at the Esso garage by the railway station. (See the town tour, starting from South Harbour, in Chapter 12.)

CHAPTER 12

WHITEHAVEN

Wellington and Duke Pits

Wellington Pit, which operated from 1840 to 1933, is still visually prominent, with its candlestick chimney, castellated walls, entrance lodge and miners' lamp house. The chimney acted as a vent and, in recent years, escaping methane has occasionally been ignited during thunderstorms. This pit used one of the largest pumping engines ever built (1866) and it was here that Whitehaven's worst mining disaster occurred in 1910 when an underground explosion killed 136 men and boys.

Below Wellington Pit and nearer the harbour lay Duke Pit, with its gigantic fan chamber (now left as a relic). The pit was sunk in 1747 by the famous local mining engineer Carlisle Spedding.

The fan chamber dates from 1862 and used to house the centrigual Guibal fan, originally developed in Belgium and patented in 1862. It had oak veins and was about 12 m (36 ft) in diameter. It was here, in 1806, that one of the most dangerous experiments in mining technology was carried out. The 'firedamp' (air containing methane) was piped to the bottom of the pit shaft and ignited to produce a ventilation current. The more traditional, but still dangerous, method was to light a coal fire at the bottom of the shaft to encourage convection currents.

WHITEHAVEN HARBOUR

This harbour is the oldest on the coast of Cumbria and has a history going back over three centuries. Christopher Lowther

The candlestick-shaped vent of Whitehaven's Wellington Pit.

began its construction in 1634 as a natural progression from the development of coal mining in the area, aiming to find a market for Cumbrian coal in Dublin. Before this the bay had served as a natural harbour, enabling the Roman Emperor Agricola to provision his advancing legions. Later, from 1125, the monks of St Bees had rights of harbourage here.

Before 1630 the bay held six cottages and one fishing boat. The first quay was the Old Quay, with its watch tower and later sundial of 1730. The original quay was lengthened in 1665 and in 1687 but part of it remains one of the oldest coal wharves in Britain.

The next stages of development were mainly along the South Harbour. Beside coal, the port was now handling trade with Virginia, Maryland and the West Indies, and shipments included rum, sugar and tobacco. Sadly, slaves were also imported via Whitehaven. One jetty in the south harbour is named Sugar Tongue, a reference to those times.

During the seventeenth century Whitehaven was a major west coast port; only Bristol had more trade. Almost all Ireland's coal was exported from Whitehaven and this trade reached its peak in the late 1920s, when 425000 tonnes was exported in a year.

Queen's Dock was constructed in 1872–6 in an attempt to overcome the tidal nature of the existing basins but this development was plagued by subsidence and cracking. However these problems were solved and the dock is still in use, though only just. The channel out to sea was kept clear for navigation by Britain's last coal-fired dredger but this, alas, has now been laid to rest.

During the Second World War a Danish fishing fleet was based on the South Harbour. Fishing activity has continued to the present day and the Sugar Tongue jetty has an ice-making plant.

Work is currently underway on the construction of the Beacon Visitor Centre on the quayside which should include interesting displays on Whitehaven's history.

Between the Sugar and Lime Tongue jetties are the remains of a patent slip for launching and removing ships from

135

the harbour. Vessels were built locally, the last wooden ship being launched in 1870.

It has been suggested that family quarrels amongst the Lowthers led them to neglect the port and this caused its decline in the nineteenth century. However competition from other Cumbrian ports like Maryport, and the growth of Liverpool and Glasgow with their greater hinterlands, were probably more important factors in Whitehaven's gradual demise as a port.

John Paul Jones

Whitehaven Harbour can claim to be the scene of the last attempted invasion of England, in 1778. Although the invasion did not succeed it significantly reduced the port's trade with America.

When he was twelve years old John Paul, a lad from Kirkbean on the Scottish side of the Solway, became an apprentice seaman to a Whitehaven shipowner. After an incident off Tobago in which his ship's carpenter died after being flogged and then knocked down with a belaying pin, he settled in America. In 1777, and now known as John Paul Jones, he was given command of the privateer, the *Ranger*, during the American War of Independence. Jones brought his ship, and others under his command, and based them in French ports. As he was ill-equipped to take on the might of the British Navy in open combat he decided to set fire to their ships in his former home waters.

On 23 April 1778, Jones landed about thirty armed men at Whitehaven. He spiked the guns of the fort (which was situated next to Duke Pit). Then he set fire to three ships in the harbour and had another 200 at his mercy. However he was betrayed by one of his men and the alarm was given.

Before any local force could muster, Jones returned to the *Ranger*. The locals quickly unspiked a couple of their guns but failed to hit the retreating Americans. The *Ranger* then veered off towards the Solway to seek further retribution from Jones's father's former employer, the Earl of Selkirk.

The *Ranger* was eventually sunk but not before Jones and

his crew had escaped, complete with spoils from his North Sea actions, to Holland.

This is said to have been one of the causes of a later war between the English and Dutch.

Although he later joined the French Navy, Americans still regard Admiral Paul Jones as the founder of the US Navy. After this raid on the port Whitehaven's defences were strengthened and a Long John canon from this era can be seen at South Beach.

WHITEHAVEN TOWN

The name *Whit-fold* (or 'White Head') was known in the twelfth century and in 1295 *Whytot-haven* is mentioned. Whilst the area was owned by St Bees Priory it became a small fishing village.

The lands eventually passed to the Lowther family in the seventeenth century. During John Lowther's ownership the population grew from 250, to over 2000 at the time of his death in 1705. Although the town's development was rapid it was also carefully thought out, and Whitehaven became the earliest example of a post-medieval planned town in England, laid out in a grid-iron pattern.

Sir John Lowther divided the grid into plots about 5 m (16 ft) wide. The builders were obliged to build their fronts above a certain height, usually at least three storeys, and their doors and windows were made to approved measurements. All buildings and warehouse were built to a multiple of the 5 m (16 ft) plot width, creating a pleasing sense of balance and proportion. (Unfortunately, during the late nineteenth and early twentieth centuries, greed led to over-intensive development and poor sanitation.)

Whilst coal and the harbour provided the lifeblood of the town in the mid-nineteenth century there were other local industries of importance. Pottery, for example, made of local clays, was exported to the US and Ireland. In addition the local, virtually phosphorus-free iron ore was used in fifty-four blast furnaces along the coast between Millom and Maryport. There was also a waterpowered mill, built to process

American cotton, and four breweries to quench the industrial thirst prevalent at the time.

Although the town grew, local churches still remained chapelries of St Bees until 1835. The Methodist John Wesley preached at Whitehaven but he preferred to approach from across the Lakes. This was because his two previous coastal journeys had left him with the impression that the local innkeepers deliberately delayed him long enough to miss the estuary crossings in favour of their trade.

A Tour of Whitehaven

Go alongside South Harbour and turn left at the end to enter West Strand. Pass the end of Sugar Tongue, cross the road to the Royal Standard, and then the Old Customs House (built in 1810–11, with a porch of Tuscan columns). Beyond this, bear right, cross the main road and go into Roper Street, on the left of Golden Lion House.

This former pub was the original Customs House and dates back to the early seventeenth century. Numbers 44 and 45 Roper Street have Georgian Gothic shopfronts. Further along on the right, numbers 36 to 40 retain some fine Georgian features, and the street contains several restored eighteenth-century houses.

Number 25, on the left, was the home of Captain Daniel Brocklebank, founder of a shipping company of that name which, in turn, became part of the famous Cunard line. Brocklebank's operated a shipyard here between 1780 and 1865. Number 30, at the end on the left, was built in 1743, by James Spedding, the son of Carlisle. The acorn on the pediment over the door is a reminder of the Spedding coat of arms but the building has had nineteenth-century details imposed on its eighteenth-century structure.

At the end turn left into Scotch Street and on your left you will see a fine terrace of early eighteenth-century merchants' houses showing the 5 m (16 ft) plot width. Union Hall, by the traffic lights, has been described as 'an essential part of Italianate Whitehaven'.

138

Cross the road and turn right into Lowther Street to pass the Civic Hall which houses the Whitehaven Museum and Art Gallery. The museum sheds light on the industrial, maritime, and social history of Whitehaven. It is open all year round, from 9 a.m. to 5 p.m. on Monday to Friday and 9 a.m. to 4 p.m. on Saturday. Admission is free.

Further along Lowther Street is Whitehaven Castle, built in its current form by Sir James Lowther in 1769. (Sir James, later the Earl of Lonsdale, made this his house in Whitehaven. It was later used as a hospital and may, by now, be turned into flats or used as council offices.)

Go back down Lowther Street, and turn right into Scotch Street with more elegant terraces, and with the 'finest house in Whitehaven', number 14, across to the left. (This mid-eighteenth-century stone building has five bays, a top balustrade, and a doorway with Ionic columns.)

Continue along Scotch Street and on your right is Duke Street.

In the lower left-hand corner of Duke Street is Somerset House (built about 1750). The Gothic porch with clustered shafts is reached by an outer stair. The house was named after the Duke of Somerset who had an estate just north of here at Bransty. One owner of this house went bankrupt when he lost ten ships and a Virginian estate during the American War of Independence.

Follow Scotch Street uphill and turn left into George Street. Continue along, then turn right into Queen Street and up to St James' Church.

This church was designed by the engineer Carlisle Spedding and built in 1752–3. Pevsner says it has 'the finest Georgian Church interior in the County'. The ceilings are attributed to the Italians Artaria and Bugatti, and the painting over the altar, *The Transfiguration*, by Guilio Procaccini, originally hung in Madrid. The pulpit is a wine-glass shape, standing on high columns, and originally had reading pews before it.

139

The galleries around three sides stand on Tuscan columns that carry influted Ionic columns. The Florentine-style Baptistry is of Sienna marble (c1650) and the altar is cedarwood decorated with gold. The sanctuary lamp is a coal miner's lamp.

> Return down Queen Street, continue over George and Duke Street and go into the gardens to the tower of St Nicholas Church Centre.

Originally a small chapel built in 1693, St Nicholas was rebuilt as a church in 1883 but destroyed by fire in 1971.

In the churchyard is the grave of Mrs Mildred Gale (there is also a plaque in the tower to her memory), the wife of George Gale, a local tobacco-dealer. They were married in Virginia but returned to Whitehaven with three children from her first marriage.

The two boys went to school at Appleby but when their mother's will was contested, in America, the boys had to return to her first husband's family. If this hadn't happened history would have been very different, for one of those boys was George Washington, the first US President.

> From the front of St Nicholas tower, turn right into Lowther Street. On your right is the 1833 Regency-style Trustees Savings Bank (complete with Doric columns and period wrought-iron balustrade) and on your left is the long-established wine firm of R. and H. Jefferson (founded on the import of rum from the West Indies to Whitehaven in 1785).
>
> Turn right down King Street, by Burton's, then left. Now turn immediately right into Tangier Street, before continuing to the railway station. On the way you pass the Waverley Hotel, once Tangier House, which was built as a mansion for Captain Richard Senhouse, whose family we shall meet later. The Shipwright's Arms, another old Whitehaven pub is also on the right. The railway station lies ahead.

CHAPTER 13

WHITEHAVEN TO WORKINGTON

LEAVING WHITEHAVEN

Just above the entrance to Whitehaven station go left.
Then turn immediately left again along the track between
the railway and the cliff. Follow this track around Redness
Point and rejoin the road.

The local outcrops of Triassic sandstone appear dismal on a
wet day but warm and colourful when the sun shines. Along
this stretch there are many signs of the past industry and
present economic hardship, yet the area is rich in wildlife and
unusual plant species. The fulmar makes the cliffs its home
and wild flowers, such as hemp agrimony, wood vetch, dyer's
greenwood and the narrow-leaved everlasting pea, are to be
found. Butterflies, like the green-veined white, frequent this
stretch, while short-eared owls and kestrels hunt between the
cliffs and the sea.

The ruins along the track, which used to be the wagonway
between this stretch of coast and the harbour, include those of
William and Henry Pits.

William Pit was sunk in 1804 and completed by 1812.
Around the turn of the century it had some 52 sq km (20 sq
miles) of under-sea workings and produced nearly 250 000
tonnes of coal per year. In the late nineteenth century they
were still using wicker hazel baskets, called corves, to haul
coal to the surface. It was here, back in 1947, that a mining
accident cost the lives of 104 men. William Pit closed in 1955.

Henry Pit had a shorter life, from 1870 to 1891, and reached a depth of 285 m (935 ft).

> Go left on the road and return to the shore, passing under the railway just short of Parton station and war memorial.

Parton

Parton ironworks were built in 1873; now only ruins mark the site. Once we noted harebells growing up through what should have been the station platform.

Now a cliffside village, the original settlement clustered round an ancient port that was extended in 1705 by the local landowner, Mr Fletcher of nearby Moresby Hall, when he built a pier to ship out his coal. It is likely that even before this it was a Roman port, serving the fort on the headland above.

Sir John Lowther didn't like competition with his financial interests in Whitehaven Harbour and successfully opposed attempts by the Fletchers and the Lamplughs to set up a harbour at Parton. Despite this, a new pier was built in 1796, only to be destroyed by a storm. Moresby coal then had to go through Whitehaven after all.

> Go along the coastline and cross Lowca Beck. Turn right under the railway, follow the far bank of the stream and walk along to meet the road. Just back and up the hill from Lowca lies Moresby. (See **Way Map 15** for this area and for an alternative route to Moresby, from Parton.)

Moresby

Overlooking Parton is St Bridget's Church, Moresby, with fine views across to the sea. The church was built in 1822–3, next to the site of an earlier church whose chancel arch still stands in the churchyard. It is one of a few churches in Cumbria dedicated to St Bridget (or St Bride) who is thought to have originated as the Irish goddess Brighida. The church, in deference to local vandals, is usually locked and its stained glass windows heavily protected.

The church and its grounds are part of the 1.5 hectare

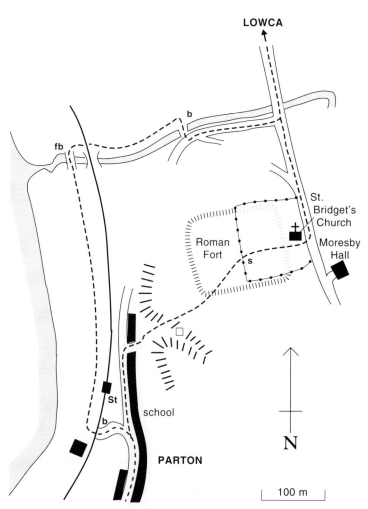

LOWCA

b

fb

Roman
Fort

s

St. Bridget's Church

Moresby Hall

St

b

school

PARTON

N

100 m

Way Map 15: Parton to Moresby

143

(4 acre) site of a Roman fort which some historians regard as the end of the Solway fortifications. (Others place the end at St Bees, whilst the historical heavyweights pronounce it to be Bowness-on-Solway.) The fort was built by the XXth legion under Hadrian in 128–138 AD.

Northwards from here is an irregular series of milecastles and turrets positioned along the coast to join Hadrian's Wall by Bowness-on-Solway. This system only becomes obvious after the next major fort at Maryport (about one day's march away). The fort at Moresby remained occupied until the fourth century.

Just across the road is a Grade I listed building, the Jacobean Moresby Hall. Pevsner describes it as: 'An eminently interesting building with a splendid facade of c1620–1700. It is all rusticated, as if it were in Bohemia.' This two-and-a-half-storey house was built onto an older structure and contains a barely recognisable pele tower with a spiral staircase. The hall annex has mullioned windows and the two parts are separated by a narrow courtyard.

The facade of Moresby Hall.

The enormous Elizabethan chimneybreast marks the possible site of the original kitchen and there are rumours of a secret passage to the church where the Fletcher family, who built the hall, are buried. After the death of the last direct heir in 1720 the hall changed hands. It was owned by two other prominant local families, the Broughams and the Lowthers, but later fell into disrepair and was used as a farmhouse.

It has now been restored as the guesthouse of a local company and no doubt offers the warm hospitality for which it was once famous, when great people came to Moresby Hall for sports and horseracing. The building is not open to the public but a good view can be gained from the road.

Lowca

Go left and continue left up the hill along the road, to pass through the village of Lowca. Continue until you see a track on your left to Park House Farm.

Beneath the reclaimed colliery spoils by Lowca Beck was the site of one of the region's most famous engineering works. The Lowca foundry was set up around 1763 by Adam Heslop to make brass cannons for local merchant vessels. The firm contined to prosper after the American War of Independence, making fittings for much-needed replacement vessels and producing machinery for the mining industry. Heslop designed and built the first rotary winding engine in the region in 1791. Another pit engine, built in the same year, is in London's Science Museum.

In 1799 Heslop formed a partnership and began to construct steam engines. During the early 1840s the firm built locomotives for the Maryport and Carlisle Railway Company and continued to make steam engines for colleries, ironworks and iron ore mines. In 1843 the first iron ship to be built in Cumberland was constructed by the firm. Two of the railway engines built by the company, *Dolgoch* (1866) and *Talyllyn* (1864), are still running on the Talyllyn Railway in Wales.

The works closed in 1921 and spoil from Lowca Colliery covered the remains. Time and money have partially healed the scars left by the tip and the tar works.

Just off the coast lies Cunning Point, a dangerous sunken crag which is exposed only during very low ebb tides. It is said to be the graveyard of an eighteenth-century pirate ship sunk one Christmas dawn. Seaward of the tip lies the coastal railway, now partially single tracked due to erosion by the sea.

Micklam coalmine once stood here. More recently it has produced clay for locally manufactured bricks, as well as the odd sack of coal. The clay was once used to make local pottery and was of sufficient quality to bring one of the famous Wedgwood family to the area.

Follow the track to Park House Farm and continue ahead through the facing gate. Bear right at a junction, and continue until you meet the track of the old mineral railway. Follow the railway track bed to the edge of Harrington where you continue down Rose Hill. Cross the railway bridge to reach Harrington Harbour.

Soon after you joined the inclined railway bed you passed into the district now called Allerdale. The name, meaning 'the dale of the River Ellen', was once that of a Norman barony and hunting forest that covered this north-western section of Cumbria.

Harrington
Harrington, (the ancient Haverington) derived its name from Hearingas who had his tribal settlement here in ancient times. It later became the seat of the Harrington family.

The quay at Harrington Harbour was built by Henry Curwen in 1760 in order to export coal from his mines. The present harbour, now used by pleasure craft and local fishermen and referred to as the marina, was also built in the eighteenth century and continued to be used by colliers until 1929.

Just south of the harbour, there was a shipyard from 1839 to 1887 and a mid-nineteenth century ironworks. The site of these demolished structures, which has now been landscaped, once rejoiced in the somewhat fanciful name 'Bellaport Marina'.

John Curwen's building of the coastal colliery in 1825 represented a major attempt to enlarge the under-sea workings. However poor management resulted in the sea breaking in and flooding the pit. Coalmining in Harrington finally ceased in the 1970s when the then National Coal Board closed No. 10 Colliery.

Harrington's church, St Mary's, has a history going back over 400 years. The font is dated 1634 but might be medieval and there is part of an Anglo-Danish cross with intertwined decoration.

Apart from another couple of interesting buildings, Harrington also has shops and refreshment facilities, should you wish to take a breather here.

Follow a track from the harbour along the coast, starting on the seaward side of the Sailing and Fisherman's Club. Continue along the track until it meets the railway line.

Where the former branch line used to climb off east, and just before the wire fencing of Workington steelworks, go under the railway and turn left. Follow the path next to the railway. This path eventually crosses the road to a private bridge to the steelworks. Continue along the path up to the road over the railway bridge. This is Bessemer Way.

WORKINGTON

The name Workington is derived either from 'the (tribal) settlement of Weorc's people' or it is a Celtic name for 'white/ clear water'. Its situation at the mouth of the River Derwent made it an ideal site for a port in Roman, Norman and medieval times.

The Derwent draws its waters from six of Lakeland's lakes (Thirlmere, Derwentwater, Bassenthwaite, Loweswater, Crummock and Buttermere). It was at the mouth of the Derwent that the monks who were carrying the body of St Cuthbert, Bishop of Lindisfarne, escaped from the Danes in 870 AD.

The remains of the buildings of Jane Pit seen on entering Workington.

Coal

Coal from local outcrops was exploited before 1650 and, as in Whitehaven, the coal industry was controlled by a local family, the Curwens of Workington Hall. However the Curwen estates were not as well organised or capitalised as those of the Lowthers.

148

One of the Curwens' collieries, Jane Pit (seen from the path alongside the railway line on your way into Workington), has had its site preserved. It was originally opened in 1843–4 and has a turreted, keep-like engine house, a battlemented chimney and a sunken horse-gin platform.

Workington Harbour

Nowadays Workington Harbour is used by ships carrying soap, phosphoric acid, railway lines and other cargoes. However it was first developed by the Lowther family in order to export coal.

The original staithes are in the mouth of the Derwent but these proved difficult for the coal vessels to reach because of river turbulence. The south bank staithes were connected to the Curwens' collieries by wagonway.

The bend in the north bank of the river was then used to make a dock basin and the Irish engineer, W. J. Doherty, built a pier into the estuary to enable larger vessels to enter the river mouth. However this development was affected by changes in the river channel. The main Lonsdale dock was built in 1864–6.

Iron

Like that of Barrow, the extraordinary growth of Workington in the 1870s was largely caused by the boom in ironmaking. The first local furnace was built in 1763 at Seaton, and the pioneer of the steelmaking process, Henry Bessemer, pioneered his new production techniques in this district.

Along with local reserves of iron ore, there were plentiful supplies of other crucial raw materials – water, limestone and coal for coke. Thus the classic reasons for industrial location and development were present, as were the local entrepreneurs. With the advent of the railways it became possible to reach a much wider market.

At their peak the three Workington furnaces were capable of producing 600 000 tonnes of iron a year. Most of the pigs were dispatched by rail to Teeside. Steel was then returned from Teeside, resmelted and rolled into heavy and light rails, fishplates, sleepers, baseplates and other fittings used in many of the world's railways.

When the blast furnaces were running the slag was tipped over the cliff, thus changing the shape of the coastline and destroying the historical site of St Michael's Mount. Some 7000 tonnes of slag were removed in the 1970s to be used as foundations for the Workington–Penrith A66 Trunk Road.

Little remains of the many local sites where iron ore was once reduced to iron. However Moss Bay, the British Steel plant, now makes high-quality railway track from steel brought in from other furnaces, a process in which it is a world leader.

This section of the route is covered by **Way Map 16.** Cross over the bridge and turn left off Bessemer Way into Lakes Road. Cross the railway lines, then turn right into Prince's Way and cross a further set of rails.

Continue along this track to the gates of the slag quarry. Turn right, go up to cross the stile and continue up the hill. Follow the track up by the edge of the quarry and bear right to reach the highest point of what used to be a slagbank and, before that, St Michael's Mount.

The local beacon, used to warn people of Scottish raids, was on St Michael's Mount. It was an old pele tower that was later whitewashed to act as a guide for incoming ships. (St Michael, though now better-known as a clothing trademark, is a patron saint of sailors.) The site was originally that of a Roman station and the tower now lies buried under the slagbank.

Descend by following the main path down the ridge towards the river mouth. Turn right along the road, pass the beehive-like building, and continue until just short of joining Curwen Road. Go down the path on your left, passing the small pool for local boats and go to cross the Derwent by the combined rail and footbridge. (The quickest way into Workington is along the right-hand quay from the nearside of the bridge. However the Way continues from the bridge in Chapter 14.)

150

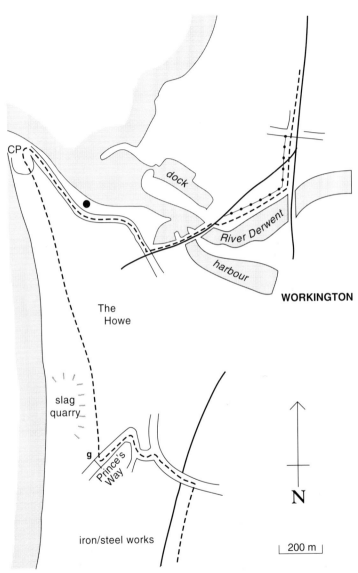

Way Map 16: Workington

151

Workington Hall

In May 1568 Mary Queen of Scots landed at Workington after her defeat at Langside. Sir Henry Curwen gave her shelter at Workington Hall and it was here that she wrote her letter of appeal to Queen Elizabeth I. As a token of thanks Mary left Sir Henry an agate cup known as 'the luck of Workington' when she departed for Cockermouth Castle. The story inspired Wordsworth to pen a sonnet on Mary Queen of Scots in his 'Poems Composed or Suggested During a Tour in the Summer of 1833'.

Workington Hall is open to the public for a limited number of hours. Check with the local Tourist Information Office (see Useful Addresses).

The building is based on a fourteenth-century pele tower and vaulted basement. During Elizabeth's reign wings were added to the earlier great hall and kitchen. Then John Christian Curwen rebuilt the Hall towards the end of the eighteenth century, using the profits from his coalmines and employing John Carr, a fashionable northern architect. The Curwen family occupied the Hall until the 1920s when they moved to the round house on Belle Isle, Windermere. Alas, during the war, soldiers were billeted here and it seems that they managed to seriously damage the building in a fire. The house was presented to the town in 1947 and, apart from some mediocre stabilising work in the 1960s and some more recent attempts to put matters right, it was left to decay until, by 1972, it had fallen into a state of ruin. This does not detract, however, from the grandeur of the building which is still worth a visit.

Helena Thompson Museum

A model of the Hall is to be found in the nearby Helena Thompson Museum (see Useful Addresses) which is housed in a mid-Georgian building where the Curwens' steward once resided. There is an interesting local history display, as well as a costume room and a Victorian Room. The museum is open every day except Sunday (10.30 am to 4 pm from April to October; 11 am to 3 pm from November to March).

To the north of the museum, and visible from it, is Schoose Farm, the home farm of Workington Hall. It was here that the Curwens and their stewards introduced pioneering agricultural practices such as zero-grazing for pit ponies, where grass was cut and brought to the ponies in order to conserve energy.

Just below the museum is the most delightful corner of Workington, Portland Square. The long, narrow, cobbled area dates from 1780 and is surrounded by well-preserved Georgian houses.

The other building of note in Workington is St John's Church in Washington Street. This was built in 1823 and its Tuscan portico is an enlarged copy of the portico designed by Inigo Jones for St Paul's in Covent Garden.

The parish church of St Michael's is on a more elevated site and includes several seventeenth-century features. It also has some earlier stonework and part of an Anglo-Danish cross shaft with interlaced decoration.

CHAPTER 14

WORKINGTON TO MARYPORT

LEAVING WORKINGTON

Cross the Derwent by the footbridge of the railway bridge (see **Way Map 16**, p. 151) and turn right to cross the rails on the edge of the dock estate. Follow the riverside path to the railway bridge and turn left on the nearside of the railway. Follow the lineside path to the road near the next bridge, opposite the liquid storage tanks.

Cross the road and go down the track, following the railway until it meets the coast at Siddick near the end of the landscaped waste heaps.

Alternatively, go left on the road, past the port entrance on your left, and then turn right along the road. Go left through the first car park to the coast. Turn right along the coastal defence and up the steps at the end of the concrete wall. From here the Way goes over the landscaped waste heaps. Take the path or track nearest the sea until you descend to the railway to meet up with the main route at Siddick.

Siddick

Inland from here lies the large pool at Siddick and the site of another undersea colliery, St Helen's. The pool is a local nature reserve, much-frequented by bird watchers, and has been designated an SSSI. Summer visitors include reed grasshopper and sedge warblers, along with tufted duck, shoveler and whitethroat; whilst in winter snipe, Bewick and whooper swans and several duck species can be seen. At times

154

of migration green and wood sandpiper, greenshank and black tern have been recorded. Peregrine, long- and short-eared owls also occur, possibly attracted here by the prospect of prey at times of large starling roosts.

East of the railway at Siddick lies the massive Iggesund Paperboard mill and the Ectona Fibres Ltd factory. Plants like these, built on greenfield sites, certainly provide much-needed jobs, but one wonders whether the impact they have on the environment might put other potential employers off the area.

Iggesund is a Swedish-owned company which manufactures cardboard used in the packaging of food, pharmaceuticals, cosmetics and cigarettes. On site there is a sawmill and pulpmill using some timber grown in the Lake District.

Ectona Fibres (which opened in 1968) makes two major products, cigarette filter tow, and polyethelene terephalate (PET) pellets which are converted into plastic bottles for carbonated drinks. Tours of the plant can be arranged for adults and children over thirteen (see Useful Addresses).

SIDDICK TO MARYPORT

From here to Maryport the route lies between the sea and the railway,the path being mostly adjacent to the railway.

Between Siddick and Flimby is a raised beach which, in season, is a cornucopia of wild flowers. Oystercatcher, ringed plover, and skylark can be seen. Here marauding crows or kestrels will be met in aerial combat by aggrieved oyster-catchers, supported by noisy though somewhat ineffectual lapwings.

Bloody cranesbill, squat patches of wild rose, sea spurge, sea rocket and various members of the hawkweed and pea families provide a feast for the eyes. Banded snails and ladybirds show themselves in this riotous display of nature – and you don't even need to stray from the path to see it.

Flimby grew alongside its mine. Whilst the township has a slightly depressing air nowadays it is nonetheless a typical mining settlement. In Wedgwood Road there is the five-bayed Allonby House (1731) and nearby Flimby Hall (1766).

Climbing the hillside behind are Flimby Woods, the only major wooded area adjacent to this section of coast. Alas it is no longer a home for herons or badgers but does contain sites of industrial archaeology.

Risehow

Risehow Farm is near the site of Roman Milefortlet 26, and Romano-British pottery from the third and fourth century has been found here. The fort suggests a continuation of the Hadrianic system south of Maryport but how far south did the system go?

> Here at Risehow the coal plant forces you towards the edge of the coast but beware of the shale hillock which is being rapidly eroded by the sea. Continue until you arrive, through the arches of a former railway embankment, at Maryport Harbour

MARYPORT

The old railway embankment around this side of the docks is another SSSI. On the embankment will be found rare flowers purple broomrape and pyramidal orchid; the small blue butterfly, with abundant supplies of its food plant, kidney vetch, can also be seen. Both the small blue butterfly and the purple broomrape are nationally rare species.

It is apt that the route should enter the town via this historic harbour, where the late L. S. Lowry spent time sketching. The mouth of the River Ellen has been used as a port since Roman times. Originally there was a village called Ellenfoot here. However in 1750, when construction of the harbour began, Humphrey Senhouse (a local landowner) renamed the town Maryport after his wife Mary Fleming, daughter of the Bishop of Carlisle.

> Through the arch, go right along the road, and turn left, with Senhouse Dock to your left.

Maryport Harbour

To the seaward side you will see the embankment, sea wall and harbour light. These were constructed below the high water mark in an attempt to make the dock independent of the tide and thus improve its viability. The 1846 harbour light is an early example of cast-iron construction.

To the right lies Senhouse Dock, now the marina. The dock was named after the Senhouse family who developed the local coalfield and then the harbour in order to export their coal. (They were to Maryport what the Lowthers were to White-haven and the Curwens to Workington.)

Senhouse dock was completed in 1884 and was mainly used to export iron railway lines and pig iron from the local furnaces. Its construction was not without its difficulties. Twice during the building of this basin great storms inundated the workings. Then, just after completion, the trend towards using wider ships meant that the entrance had to be widened.

Go back along to the south end of Elizabeth Dock to reach the *Flying Buzzard*.

Elizabeth Dock, Maryport.

This dock, which opened in 1857, was named after Humphrey Senhouse II's eldest daughter and was the first wet, non-tidal dock in Cumberland. The Maryport and Carlisle Railway had been completed, with an extension to Whitehaven, just before the opening. This brought in more coal traffic and greater use of the harbour although much of the coal still came from the local Senhouse mines.

Moored on the Elizabeth Dock is the former River Clyde steam-powered tug the *Flying Buzzard* (see Useful Addresses). From Easter to October visitors can be taken on a guided tour, at minimal coast, and on some days the ship's engines are run. Fishing boats use this basin.

The opening of the dock in Workington, which could take larger ships, coincided with the closure of Maryport ironworks in 1927. These two events, combined with the decline of local coalmining, led to the gradual demise of the harbour. It officially closed in 1961 – only a trickle of coastal shipping in coal and fish, particularly during the war, had been keeping the port going. Now regeneration is the name of the game.

Turn along the quayside to reach the River Ellen and turn right, passing the pub and café to reach the bridge.

This bridge is quite recent. Until the 1980s there was a footbridge which occupied the pillars of an 1845 swing bridge. The channel had been deepened and this removed the ford that once carried the main Carlisle to Whitehaven highway. Just south of the bridge is a grid of large wooden planks on which ships rested at low tides to have their hulls cleaned and repaired. From the bridge, to your right, is the inlet of the former Ritson's shipyard, from which, due to the narrowness of the channel, ships were launched broadside on. Such launches began in 1809 and the last took place in 1914.

Crossing the River Ellen we come to the Maritime Museum and Tourist Information Centre. Originally the Queen's Head Inn, it was rebuilt in 1881.

The museum is staffed by knowledgeable local people and it tells the story of Maryport Harbour through old photographs and paintings. Exhibits include everything from a whale's tooth to a blunderbuss, and there is a special display about Fletcher Christian (of mutiny on the *Bounty* fame). It is open from 10 a.m. to 5 p.m. from Monday to Saturday between Easter and October. Opening hours are restricted out of season – phone for details (see Useful Addresses).

Turning right over the bridge we come to Mote Hill, once the site of Roman and Norman strongholds.

W. G. Collingwood, in *The Lake Counties*, refers to the mound as Castle Hill or Pudding Pie Hill. He says it was a moated mound and may have been the site of a king's burial. Alas the only bones found under the mound were those of a heifer and colt. The historian also refers to the site as a Pre-Norman berg and mentions the importance attached to the river harbour in early medieval days, as it formed the junction of Roman roads from Bowness, Carlisle and Workington.

Just below Mote Hill lies Paper Mill Green, where Humphrey Senhouse's short-lived paper mill was situated in 1756. On the south-east side of the hill, by a loop in the river, used to stand an iron furnace built in 1752. This was the first Cumberland furnace to use coke. The hill lies very close to a fault line that separates the coal measures stretching to the south and east and the underlying Triassic sandstone to the north.

At the time of writing, a heritage park is proposed alongside the River Ellen. Features include reconstructions of the eighteenth-century shipyard and a Roman galley.

Go back past the museum, cross Senhouse Street and enter King Street where you will see the quayside Christ Church, dated 1872. The anchor outside the church was 'caught' by a local fishing boat in the Solway and is now dedicated to Maryport seafarers lost at sea.

Outside Christ Church is the North Quay wall, the oldest surviving part of the harbour. It continues as Tongue Pier and, across the harbour to the right, is North Pier. The area between the two piers was William Wood's shipbuilding yard, the first to be established in the town in 1765. The patent slipway is buried under the shingle.

The Old Customs House and Harbour Office of 1838 are now occupied as a private house (3 North Quay) with a once beautiful porch. Alongside Christ Church is King Street, where number 13, a three-storey dwelling, has been well preserved as a mid-nineteenth-century house. At one time the site was occupied by a boot- and shoe-maker who, until 1791, displayed a light in a window to guide ships into the harbour.

Maryport Town

Go back to the church and left along King Street until you can turn right into Wallace Lane. Climb the zig-zag Market Steps, all 109 of them. Then continue up, along Eaglesfield Street, and into Fleming Square.

This was the town's former market square whose cobbles were likened, by Charles Dickens, to kidney beans. The square used to have a central market hall, where butter was sold, but this undistinguished building was demolished in the 1950s. The surrounding Georgian and Victorian houses create a scene of elegance, enhanced by some of the conservation work that has been carried out.

Like Whitehaven, Maryport was designed on a grid pattern in the mid-eighteenth century. However the town was never fully developed according to the plans.

Turn left as you enter the square and leave by the top left-hand corner. Follow this road along, across High Street and then right along the top of the Sea Brows to the site of the Roman fort of Alauna in the field behind the museum.

The Romans in Maryport

The Romans arrived in this Celtic-speaking region in around 79 AD under Agricola. The coast was important as a supply line to their occupying forces and also served as a defensive frontier. Like the port at Ravenglass, Maryport was vital both to receive supplies and as a base for possible invasions of Scotland and Ireland.

From Maryport there was a line of mileforts (a Roman mile being 1480 m/1620 yds) and fortlets (at 494 m/540 yd intervals) all the way to Hadrian's Wall at Bowness-on-Solway. The other major forts to the south of Bowness were Kirkbride, Beckfoot, Maryport, Burrow Walls (Workington), Moresby (north of Whitehaven) and Ravenglass.

After Roman altars were found here in 1870 the fort site was extensively excavated by the Senhouse family. They took some stone for building even though there was an adjacent quarry. However they preserved the altars and some sculptures, along with other marked stones, and took them to their house, Netherhall, for safe-keeping. The fort was built around 122–3 AD in the early years of Hadrian's Emperorship (117–138). It appears to have been occupied until 400 AD and was built at the same time as the fortlets going northwards from here to Moricambe Bay.

In 1990 the Battery, which once had guns pointing out to sea and was used in civil defence training, was refurbished as a museum. It now displays the altar stones, together with reconstruction models and paintings of Roman life at the fort. Indeed it boasts the largest collection of Roman sculpture from a single site in Britain. Seventeen altars have been found, of which sixteen bear inscriptions. They were dedicated by the commanders of the fort each January when the auxilaries renewed their oaths of allegiance to the Emperor. The Senhouse Roman Museum is open from April to October, every day except Monday and Wednesday, from 10 a.m. to 5 p.m. Opening hours are restricted out of season – phone for details (see Useful Addresses).

Outside the museum there are fine views across the Solway to southern Scotland. The fort was thus well situated both for defence and for keeping watch over the Roman vessels in Ellenfoot harbour.

From the museum, descend gently northwards to rejoin the promenade. The West Cumbrian Coast is now behind you, and it's on around the Solway to Carlisle and the Borders.

SECTION FIVE
THE SOLWAY COAST AND HADRIAN'S WALL

From Maryport Sea Brows the character of the Irish Sea coast gives way to that of the Solway. We are now on a stretch of coast designated as an Area of Outstanding Natural Beauty (AONB) since 1964 and covering some 107 sq km (41 sq miles). To quote the 1949 National Parks and Countryside Act, the idea behind AONBs is 'to preserve and enhance the natural beauty . . .' However tourist pressures, large caravan sites and low-key official backing for conservation mean that the landscape is still under threat to some extent.

Nevertheless oystercatchers stand facing the wind and add their calls to those of the sandpipers, Cormorants fly low along the crests of breakers, whilst curlews fly to and from the shore, and wheatears flit amongst the dune vegetation.

The characteristic feature of this section of coastline is the continuous raised beach caused by changes in sea level and a bit of land that may still be slowly rising. The wave-cut beaches represent the coastline as it was before the sea level changed. Most of this beach is around 8 m (26 ft) high but an older line of sea cliffs can sometimes be noted, as at Swarthy Hill. Along here sea holly, ragwort, coltsfoot and feverfew are found in abundance, as are many motorists who tend to sit pasty-faced in their cars.

After Grune Point the Way goes round its last major corner, further from the influence of the Irish Sea and towards the more estuarine character of the Solway's tributaries the Eden and the Esk.

Grune Point is the product of longshore drift, in which currents have built a finger of land into Moricambe Bay. Around the bay are superb examples of tidal mud flats and saltmarshes where geomorphology and fauna vividly interact.

Between Roman withdrawal from Britain and the arrival of the first Anglian colonists, the Solway was the centre of the Kingdom of Rheged. For three centuries after the reign of Edward I raids and counter-raids across the Scottish border were a part of everyday life for local people, causing them to build numerous pele towers (as at Newton Arlosh and Burgh churches) in which to take shelter.

Many raids took place down the coast. Most notable was one in 1316 when the Scots poured into the Furness area and one in 1322 when two armies swept down into Cumbria with one getting as far as Lancashire.

The sixteenth century was the period when cross-border family feuds and raids reached their peak. For many of these families the border did not physically exist and they changed their allegiances to suit the prevailing political situation. Nonetheless they were times of great unease and few could sleep peacefully in their beds for fear of the border reivers coming to take cattle, sheep and horses, often inflicting injury or death on anyone who resisted. G. MacDonald Fraser (see Bibliography) gives a very readable account of these turbulent times.

The Act of Union, signed in 1706, gradually brought peace to the region. With peace came a degree of prosperity and for the first time farmers could afford to build their houses and outbuildings in stone.

The Solway was once bridged, from Bowness to Annan, by a railway viaduct which, apart from its embankments, is now no more. Other disused railway bridges over roads, listed today by the Department of the Environment as examples of industrial archeology, often form the highest points in the landscape. Unless you go inland to Carlisle the only way to cross to Scotland is by the old fords (called *waths*) but this is not advised.

Sulwath (meaning 'the muddy ford'), which was situated on the eastern part of the estuary, gave rise to the present name Solway. Other fords existed on the Eden and Esk, the two main tributaries of the Solway Firth. Examples of these were at Etterby, Grinsdale, Rockcliffe, Stonewath and Peatwath by Old Sandsfield (where Edward I crossed to hammer the Scots and where 900 of Alexander II's men died after a raid on Holme Cultram Abbey). One of the few fords that crossed the estuary itself was Bowness Wath, which went from Bowness to Annan and was used by Wallace, Edward I and Robert of Winchelsea (an Archbishop of Canterbury who travelled the region as a peacemaker during the border troubles).

All seems quiet now by the Solway. Shrimps are collected by the northern shore and salmon are caught in the estuary by the age-old method of *haaf* netting, although this is no longer common. (*Haaf* is Norse for 'channel'.) The other method is fixed nets. Fishing rights appear to have been apportioned in relation to the ground held by the adjacent landowners, some of whom were monastic. G. Neilson gives details in his *Annals of the Solway Until A.D. 1307* (see Bibliography).

In early summer the marsh fritillary butterfly inhabits the fringes of the Solway Firth. But from a wildlife point of view it is in winter, when the local bird population is swelled by migrant geese, duck and waders from more northern climes, that the area is at its best. Up to seventy-five species have been seen but the pinkfoot goose is the major visitor.

The winds bite in this part of the world but the rainfall is relatively low. Indeed the Cumbrian coast has much less precipitation than central Lakeland – another good reason to walk this route.

As it goes inland, the Solway Firth becomes increasingly narrow and this results in a rapid tidal bore. Although not very high it is very rapid – 'faster than a man on horseback' being the local saying. Under some conditions it can come over the bank and across the Way – as we found one February as we waded through waist-deep water to reach the safety of a wooded bluff.

In this area the Way still has strong links with the Hadrian defences. From Bowness we shall be walking next to the wall, along the proposed Hadrian's Wall National Trail.

There are also literary connections. The Victorian novelist Sir Walter Scott based parts of his work around the Cumbrian Coast, particularly along the Solway.

CHAPTER 15

MARYPORT TO SILLOTH

MARYPORT TO ALLONBY

From Maryport Roman Museum go north along the tarred path. When it forks, go left, down to the promenade. Walk along the promenade until it finishes at Bank End Farm, then follow the seaward edge of Maryport Golf Course. Beyond the golf course continue on the raised beach, between the road and the sea, past the road junction to Crosscanonby (with toilets on the right). Pass Saltpans, with a viewing point on the drumlin above the car park, and continue on the raised beach to Allonby.

Crosscanonby

Crosscanonby lies just a short distance off the Way and for those with an interest in architecture and small churches it is certainly worth a diversion. From the drumlin on which the settlement is situated this fine Norman Church looks out towards the Solway. It dates from around 1100 AD but incorporates Roman masonry such as the superb chancel arch stones reset from the fort of Alauna at Maryport. There are also several pre-Norman sculptures, including a tenth-century cross-shaft decorated with dragons but without any interlaced patterns. A Danish hogback tombstone outside the church, provides further evidence that a place of worship existed here before the coming of the Normans.

Saltmaking is a traditional Cumbrian industry and saltpans were often operated commercially by local abbeys and priories. Several places along the Way have names which indicate that they were once saltmaking sites – Salthouse, Saltom, Salta and Saltcoates. Salt was a valuable source of income for manorial and monastic landowners. The saltpans on the coast below Crosscanonby were built around 1650 by the Senhouse family and were coal-fired. They operated until 1736.

A large cobble wall circle with clay infill, sometimes with added peat, acted as a filter called a sleech pit or kinch. After high tides salt-laden sand (sleech) was brought from the shore by a horse-drawn rake (a hap) and piled up in the kinch. When full, sea water was poured over and the brine would trickle into the brine pit. When the brine was concentrated enough to float an egg, the solution would be slowly evaporated in iron pans to produce large salt crystals. Other mineral salts were also reclaimed from the pan.

Saltmaking was taxable from 1696 to 1824 and the local salt officer was based at Netherhall. Immediately south of the pans is the ash heap, whilst the foundations of the cottages and stables are over the road. At times the industry could not keep pace with demand and so local boats, from Powfoot, Parton, Whitehaven, Workington and Ravenglass, for example, would sell salted fishing catches to Chester and Liverpool and return with purchased cargoes of salt.

Next to the car park is an information board about the cottages and, if you go up the steps to the viewpoint, you will find a further board which explains how the salt was made.

Adjacent to the car park, on Swarthy Hill, is the site of Roman Milefortlet 21. Following excavations started in 1990, this is now open to the public. The excavations were con-ducted with the help of American volunteers and the first season's dig revealed detailed information about the internal layout of this series of fortlets. Such fortlets were designed to hold a substantial garrison on a permanent basis but this one was possibly only occupied from 222 to 380 AD.

The route to Allonby is somewhat marred by caravan sites, silo towers and galvanised-iron constructions. Even so, there are interesting plants to be seen. Look out for the sea holly, the yellow-horned poppy and the Isle of Man cabbage.

Looking southwest towards Maryport from the site of the Roman fort at Swarthy Hill.

Allonby

Allonby village was a popular sea bathing resort in the mid-eighteenth century. It also had a fleet of fifty herring fishing vessels but now only a few individuals set lines for skate, cod or flounder.

In 1802 the village was still being described in *The Beauties of England and Wales*, as a 'neat well built town resorted to in the summer season'. Charles Dickens visited in 1857 but the place did not live up to his expectations of the 'most delicious piece of sea coast to be found.' Instead he found 'a small, unruly, outlandish place, rough stone houses in half mourning . . .' Dickens came here with Wilkie Collins during the tour described in 'A Tale of Two Idle Apprentices'.

Allonby has a pretty cobbled main street and stream. The only formal buildings are North Lodge (early nineteenth century) and the former sea-water baths of 1835. However the village has a cluster of attractive buildings and deserves its Conservation Area status. Many of the houses are good examples of vernacular architecture but it is the grouping rather than the individual buildings that gives the settlement its character.

Although its heyday was in the nineteenth-century Allonby is still a popular place for refreshment and seabathing. There are ponies for hire, and the putting green offers a real challenge as you try to navigate the golf balls around rough grass and horse dung!

Like Beckfoot and Cardurnock further along the Way, Allonby has a submerged forest off the coast. However this is only revealed at very low tides and, possibly, with the right tidal scouring of the sands.

ALLONBY TO SILLOTH

Continue along the raised beach from Allonby, crossing the stream by the footbridge. Go to Seacroft Farm where you will have to round Dubmill Point on the roadside sea defences. The landward side of the beach can be used at low tide but please remember that the birds are easily disturbed.

Salta Moss SSSI

Just inland from Seacroft Farm lies Salta Moss, a 62 hectare (153 acre) SSSI. It consists of old peat moss with pond and reed swamp and has a varied and interesting bird population, including short-eared owls. Such peat areas are becoming rarer, as they have too often been turned to agricultural use; hence the need to protect those areas that remain. Owls and roe deer can sometimes be seen on Salta Moss.

There are several small wet areas rich in wildlife along the coastal stretch. Many are the result of glacial drift and local alluvium leaving poorly drained hollows.

Beyond Dubmill Point, where the road branches slightly from the shore, cross the stile ahead. Go to the finger post, turn left to reach the shore, then follow this north, keeping dogs on a lead. Cross a footbridge to arrive opposite the track from Mawbray village.

Mawbray Bank SSSI

From Dubmill Point almost all the way to Silloth our route takes us through the Silloth Dunes and Mawbray Bank SSSI. Excluding a narrow area around Beckfoot this stretch of dunes is almost 8 km (5 miles) long. This is one of three such dune systems in West Cumbria. Biologists will recognise the transition from vegetated shingle bank, through mobile and fixed dunes, to dune grassland and maritime heath – a fine example of succession. The rare natterjack toad and great crested newts have been found in the area, along with vegetation typical of the different habitats across the succession. Around Wolsty Bank you might see a display of northern marsh orchids, whilst further north the Mediterranean tassel hyacinth blooms and the natterjack toad has been sighted. These are fragile habitats. The less trampling the better so please stick to paths or use the beach.

Upper Solway Flats and Marshes SSSI

Seaward of Dubmill Point and almost all of the remainder of the Way to Carlisle lies a further SSSI – the Upper Solway

From Dubmill Point onwards the views north across the Solway are dominated by Criffel.

Flats and Marshes. This covers an area of almost 30000 hectares (74000 acres) and reaches from Dubmill across to the Scottish shore. It includes the whole estuary and most of the adjacent saltings. However the first real place to appreciate this SSSI is Grune Point, Skinburness. Here birdwatchers have recorded pink-footed and barnacle geese, oystercatcher, knot, lapwing, dunlin, golden plover and bar-tailed godwit, along with wigeon, mallard, teal, pintail, shelduck and the ubiquitous cormorant.

Mawbray

Mawbray, as the walker will notice, was once the site of extensive sand and gravel extraction from the raised beach. The village of Mawbray, a Conservation Area, is situated slightly inland. The site was once that of a grange farm of Holme Cultram Abbey and, at the beginning of this century, a stone effigy of a warrior was discovered here. It was thought to represent Robert Bruce who was buried at the Abbey. The village pub, the Lowther Arms, is the only pub between Allonby and Silloth.

Nikolaus Pevsner believed that the sea had claimed two churches north of here. Part of the Roman line of forts may also have been inundated.

Continue ahead, along the path through the seaward side of the raised beach. When you reach Beckfoot you have to cross the stream by the road bridge. Regain the open green by taking the next path to the left.

Beckfoot

Beckfoot Roman fort was a 19 km (12 mile) walk from Maryport (about one day's march). The fort site covers slightly more than 1 hectare (2½ acres) and is almost the smallest garrison of the Hadrianic defences. It was called Bribra. Its walls were 2 m (6½ ft) thick and it was backed by internal, rectangular towers. Minor traces of a civil settlement lie south-east of the fort.

At exceptionally low tides the remains of a submerged

forest can be seen. This was probably a hazel wood some 6000 years ago.

> Continue by the raised beach. From the Wolsty Bank area keep to the beach at low tide until you reach a wooden-edged path opposite a small lighthouse and just after a large wild rose thicket on the dunes. Take this path inland, up to a cinder track. Go directly across the golf course, using a track over the links. Pass a gate, then veer slightly left towards some houses, as the path goes to meet the road. Follow the road left and cross over the former railway. Then turn left to go left down the granite-setted street to the Green, the heart of Silloth. Alternatively, once you reach the golf course path, keep to the seaward side and enter Silloth by the edge of the docks.

Silloth

Silloth (once *Sea-lath*, 'the barn by the sea') was part of the grange farm of Holme Cultram Abbey. When the abbey was dissolved in 1538 its open field farming system of some 220 hectares (544 acres) was purchased by a Robert Wheatley who leased out parcels to tenant farmers. These farmers elected to continue using the old communal system and, such was its success, that a further 176 hectares (435 acres) of land was added.

Silloth was connected to Carlisle by rail in 1856 in order to serve as a port for the manufacturers of the city. It was also developed as a holiday resort, with a grid-iron pattern of streets culminating in the wide promenade of Criffel Street. The result was full of Victorian elegance and today, caravans and amusement arcades aside, it modestly fulfils its original function. A few Scots, whose forefathers may have been border reivers from across the Solway, join the visitors. It is a place where people come for their summer holidays dressed for winter.

Following the demise of Port Carlisle, Silloth Dock opened in 1858. Today it deals mainly in cattle and grain, as indicated by the flour mill nearby. A visitor centre is being considered.

CHAPTER 16

SILLOTH
TO KIRKBRIDE

SILLOTH TO ABBEYTOWN

From the seafront promenade by Silloth's Green go north.
Continue next to the road and keep seaward of the houses
at Skinburness when the road bends slightly right. Pass in
front of the houses along Skinburnessbank and continue
along the track until it bends right. Go through the gate
ahead of you and along the path to Grune Point.

Grune Point

Skinburness is said to mean 'the headland of the demon-
haunted castle', the headland being Grune Point. It was here,
according to an American professor, that Sir Gawain had his
fateful meeting with the Green Knight. It was also the scene of
Bonnie Prince Charlie's meeting with the Jacobites after
Culloden in Sir Walter Scott's *Redgauntlet*.

Slight terraced steps, which can be seen as you walk along,
show that the shingle of Grune is gradually building up and
extending the headland. Old maps and measurements of the
relative positions of Roman milecastles add evidence that
longshore drift is still adding to the coastline here.

To the east of Grune Point are the windswept levels of
Moricambe Bay. Around the bay are flat marshes where
hedges and trees only survive in sheltered spots.

In 1988 Grune, with its varied flora and bird life, became
part of the larger Upper Solway Flats and Marshes SSSI. The
flats and marshes of the Upper Solway Firth form one of the

largest continuous inter-tidal habitats in Britain, only exceeded in size by Morecambe Bay and the Wash. The whole
estuarine complex is a site of national and international
importance for wintering wildfowl and wading birds, as it
forms a vital link in a chain of west coast estuaries used by
migrating birds. The site is also noted for its populations of
natterjack toads and invertebrates, whilst the geomorphology
and vegetation of the estuarine saltmarshes or merses are also
of great importance. (Broad transitions to mature upper-
marsh are particularly well represented.) A number of rare
plant species and notable geological exposures, mostly on the
northern shores, also occur here.

Plant species that can be seen around Grune include sea
holly, burnet rose, bloody cranesbill, the Isle of Man cabbage
and Dyer's greenweed. The point is also a super place to watch
the tides. The wartime look-out shelter has been rebuilt in
Buddhist stupa style, as a memorial to four local people who
drowned while trying to rescue wildfowlers in difficulty.

Grune Point once held a chapel of St John. There are no
signs of the chapel now although its existence is recorded on
large-scale O.S. maps. Its graveyard is now a grazing field. Its
usage probably greatly diminished after a storm in the early
fourteenth century which saw the end of Skinburness port and
the removal of the population to Newton Arlosh.

Go along the bayside of Grune Point to reach a track.
Follow this track to a road junction where you turn left.

Skinburness Port
Edward I gathered a fleet for the invasion of Scotland at the
port of Skinburness in 1299–1300. With a company of about
fifty ships he sheltered in the lee of the point, awaiting an
opportune moment to confront the Scots, led by Wallace, and
seize the land around the Solway for England. Edward later
granted the town of Skinburness charters for a market and
fair.

In 1301 the port was destroyed in a great storm, along with
much of the village. Four years later the landowners, the

monks of Holme Cultram Abbey, built Newton Arlosh to replace Skinburness. South of Skinburness, the embankment we cross was built to protect Silloth Grange, the abbey farm, from the depredations of the sea.

On the road, climb immediately left up the sea dyke, then down to pass over a gated bridge and enter Skinburness Marsh. This is a permissive route, so dogs *must* be kept on a lead. At times of very high tides, the saltmarsh will be underwater. Follow the waymarked route across the saltings. Bridges are used to cross the dykes that feed into Skinburness Creek. At times of exceptional high tide or fog the Skinburness to Calvo and Abbeytown road should be used instead.

After the bridge near the fence the route goes parallel to the right-hand fence to cross a stile. From here the rough route goes round near the enclosed fields. The key is to keep the longer vegetation to the right. After East Border Farm keep near the right-hand boundary to cross a stile. Then walk along the saltings associated with the River Waver.

The next section of the route is shown on **Way Map 17**. Follow the track along a short section of the river bank until a gravel path goes off to your right to join the road. Follow the gravel path, then go left on the road to cross Rumbling Bridge. Rejoin the river bank (a footpath sign says Abbeytown) and follow it along to cross a stile and then a footbridge. Cross the field to the left of the overhead electrical wires, and cross the plank footbridge and stile. Go up the right-hand boundary of the field, through the gate in the corner. Continue in this direction, by the right-hand hedge in the second large field, until a gate gives access to a track leading down to Abbeytown.

Near the footbridge where you leave the river is the site where St Christian's Chapel once stood. It probably only served for a short period due to constant raids by the Scots.

All around us the flat landscape commemorates the

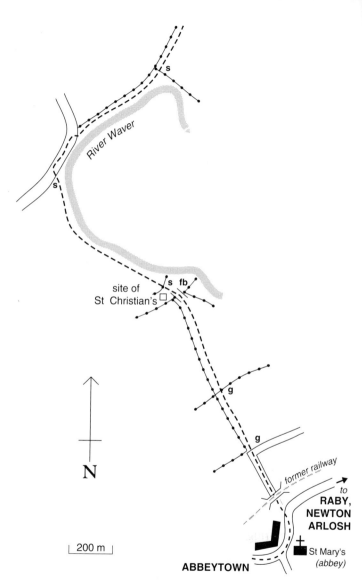

Way Map 17: Abbeytown

178

pioneers of monastic times who reclaimed wet lands through drainage. Old trees are bent by the wind and new ones fight to survive in the inhospitable, salty draughts. The saltmarshes also produce Cumberland turf which is not only a favourite for lawns and bowling greens but also graces the centre court at Wimbledon and the football pitch at Wembley Stadium. The sea-washed turf is a reminder that the Norse practice of transhumance still takes place – Lakeland Herdwicks and Swaledales from the high fells are brought down here to graze in the winter.

Some of the marshes are accumulating as the sea deposits alluvium, while others are being eroded. The coastline is ever-changing.

Abbeytown

Abbeytown was the village of Holme Cultram Abbey. The abbey ruins apart, there is little to see. The historian W. G. Collingwood mentions a moated mound to the north of the church which he called a *berg*, whilst Nikolaus Pevsner refers to it as a *mote*. Pevsner also comments on Millgrove House (dated 1664), an almshouse some 200 m (220 yds) from the church down the Wigton road. It is a two-storey dwelling with mullioned bow windows and is well worth a minor detour.

The word *holme* means 'island' and much of this area would have been surounded by sea and marsh in prehistoric times. In 1130 AD the Scots occupied most of Cumbria and later, in 1150, Prince Henry, son of King David of Scotland, established Holme Cultram. As at Furness, the monks were Cistercians. In many ways Holme Cultram's history and prosperity were intertwined with the relationship between Scotland and England. The monks owned lands on both sides of the Solway, as well as more distant parcels in the Eden valley and the Lakeland fells.

Holme Cultram Abbey was originally a daughter house of Melrose Abbey across the Solway, from whence its first monks arrived. The monks were essentially farmers but were also involved with saltmaking and the iron trade (being granted an ore mine and furnace at Whitehaven) as well as land reclamation around the Solway. Despite suffering several Scots raids, the abbey grew to be the wealthiest in Cumberland.

During one raid in 1216 the abbey was burnt. The *Chronicle of Melrose* records that those Scots who escaped the vengeance of God, by which 1900 were drowned re-fording the Eden, were punished by their King, Alexander II.

The Earl of Carrick was buried here in 1294 (his tombstone is one of several on display) but that did not stop his son, Robert the Bruce, from plundering the abbey in 1319.

In the fourteenth century the monks built nearby Wolsty Castle as a defence against 'thiefs that came from across the water'. Only the foundations and moat remain. The books of the wizard Michael Scott were once preserved here.

Henry II of England eventually took the abbey under his wing but ecclesiastically it was still under the rule of Melrose.

One monk, Gawen Borrodaile, was suspected of poisoning an Abbot elect and was tried. With the help of powerful friends he was freed and later returned as Abbot himself. Shortly after came the Dissolution and Gawen became the first priest of Holme Cultram parish church. Part of the Abbey was left standing as the parish church because the villagers begged Thomas Cromwell to leave it as a defence for them against the Scots.

The church tower fell during repairs in 1604 when a workman lost his chisel. Whilst searching for it with a candle he set fire to a jackdaw's nest and caused the tower to collapse. The church then lay neglected for the next few centuries and suffered further decay. The parish church of St Mary was however restored in 1884–5 and is now one of four Cistercian abbey churches still in use.

The present church only occupies part of the original site. (The original was said to be so large that seven priests could say Mass without interrupting each other.) The nave, built in the late twelfth century, used to be three bays longer, and the arcade openings had two tiers of arched windows.

The west facade is still dominated by the porch built by Abbot Chambers in the early sixteenth century but the main

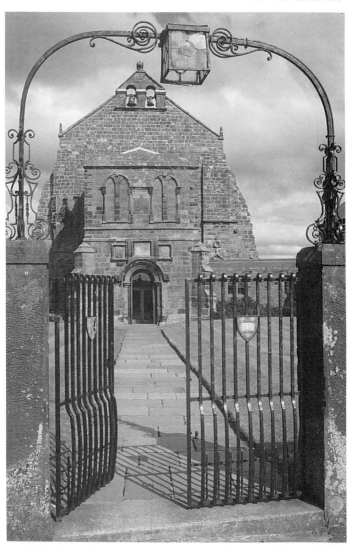

Holme Cultram church.

gable is thought to be Georgian. Part of Chambers' tomb is preserved and can be recognised by the pun on his name, a chained bear. The old pulpit, a carved niche and a carving of Henry VII can be seen inside the church.

Just down the Silloth road from Holme Cultram Abbey lies the Wheatsheaf Inn which serves meals.

ABBEYTOWN TO KIRKBRIDE

Take the road out of Abbeytown and turn left at the crossroads at Raby, having passed over the River Waver. Pass Raby Grange and the entrance to Raby Cote to arrive at the saltings where the road bends right.

Raby Cote Farm

Raby Cote Farm was originally a Holme Cultram Abbey grange farm. The occupants would have kept watch for the Scots who sailed up the creeks on the tide.

The current house dates from around the beginning of the seventeenth century and was built of stones taken from Holme Cultram Abbey. The grange would originally have had grazing fields and some desirable arable land (possibly reclaimed saltings). At the front of the house there is a long, late-medieval inscription that has been built in upside down. It comes from the abbey, as does the shield of Abbot Chambers on a relief panel. On the west front the shield of Edward the Confessor is to be found. In the sixteenth century the farm became the seat of the Chambers family and remained so for 200 years. The house is private.

There were also some saltpans with the grange (a nearby farm is called Salt Coats). Each pan owner would also have held the right to dig peat in order to fire the crystallisation pan.

The route now follows the road into the village of Newton Arlosh.

Newton Arlosh

Newton Arlosh ('the new town on the marsh') was built in 1305 to replace the storm-devasted port of Skinburness. It was set up by a charter under Edward I but, with the Scottish raids and the exposed terrain, it failed to prosper. The silting of the channel was also a problem. It has been suggested that there was already a church on this site. This was believed to have been an oratory erected by St Ninian in around 400 AD to thank God for his safe return from Rome where he had been studying.

The cross-border raids dictated the style of the present-day church which was built in 1303–4 with a pele tower adjoining the nave. This heavily defensive structure was built to serve as both a house of prayer and a tower of refuge. The church is less than 9 m × 4 m (30 ft x 13 ft), whilst the tower has massive walls to withstand repeated assaults. The windows of the tower are high and narrow and there is no outer doorway. At ground level it is tunnel vaulted and at the top a turret projects on corbels. On the first floor of the tower, reached by a stone spiral staircase, is a 'priest's room', complete with large fireplace and secret chamber. Access to the top floor was

The pele tower of Newton Arlosh church is a reminder of the days of Scots raids over the border.

gained by a ladder and this was no doubt used as a place from which to pour boiling oil on the raiders.

The main door was only 68 cm (27 inches) wide, to prevent attackers rushing in. However this also meant that during weddings the bride or groom could only leave one at a time. This gave rise to the local story that whoever emerged first would be the 'boss'.

The church, dedicated to St John, was serviced by the monks until the Dissolution. The church lead was then taken to make saltpans and the church itself fell into decay. It was restored in 1843–4 and enlarged in 1894 at a cost of £320, and the ornate plasterwork inside dates from this period.

The church lectern is a carved chestnut eagle and the base, carved as a palm tree and once part of the pulpit, is made from local bog oak. The font is early thirteenth century and came from Holme Cultram Abbey.

Before the Dissolution all tenants of the parish were required to render 'boon service' to the Abbot in accordance with their landholding. For three days' work they received seventeen white herrings, a dried cod, a quarter salmon, three wheaten loaves, three loaves of yeoman's bread and three gallons of ale. In addition all tenants and their wives were given dinner by the Abbey at Christmas.

> Our route goes along the road, through the village of Newton Arlosh. It then branches right at a junction where you will see the Joiner's Arms public house. The straight road bends left where the Solway Junction Railway once ran. Go over the bridge, then down to join the fields by the first gate on the left (signed to Kirkbride).

Wedholme Flow
Just inland, and partially visible from the bridge, is Wedholme Flow, an extensive area of peat moss that is cut and sold for a range of horticultural and agricultural uses. It is a great pity that such a scarce resource and rare habitat is being destroyed for the sake of commercial gain. None of these products is essential and they are removed at the cost of rare ecosystems which, once lost, are very difficult to recreate.

The next section of the walk is shown on **Way Map 18**. Go along the right-hand field edge, cross the fenced railway track bed ahead and continue in the same direction through the rough garden. In the far right-hand corner go right, cross the stile and follow the banking to the next stile. Cross this and turn right. Then follow the right-hand fence and dyke through several fields, as the route cuts back to recross the railway track bed.

Gibbs Meadow SSSI
This next stretch of the walk is along the boundary of Gibbs Meadow SSSI, so designated because it is herb-rich meadowland. Here is a mixture of wet and dry grasslands which were traditionally cut for hay and fen vegetation, found alongside the numerous dykes. The whole site is only 10 m (33 ft) above sea level and lies on dark, peaty soils on top of alluvium.

After passing the former aircraft hangers, still by the right-hand boundary, cross the access road and a stile. The path now follows Monk's Dyke (part of one of the monks' reclamation schemes?) and emerges, via a short lane, in Kirkbride.

Kirkbride
St Bridget was the sister of St Patrick and the name Kirkbride is a Celtic inversion of 'Bridget's church'. Situated by the mouth of the River Wampool, which flows into Moricambe Bay, Kirkbride parish contains ancient British, Roman and Anglo-Saxon artefacts. For readers of Sir Walter Scott's *Redgauntlet*, it was here that *Jumping Jenny* landed her smuggled cargo and from this village that Alan Fairford started his night ride.

Continue along the road, past the Bush Inn (which serves meals). Then leave the main road to follow Church Road to the interesting St Bride's parish church, on the highest land for many a mile.

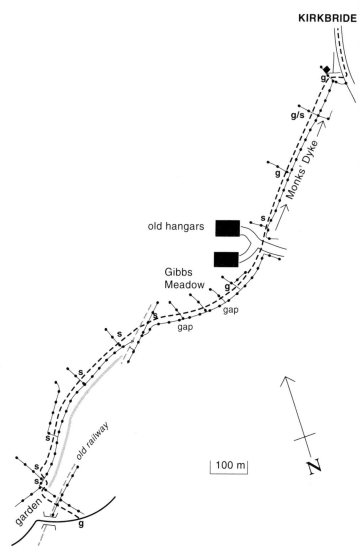

KIRKBRIDE

g/

g/s

Monks' Dyke

g

s

old hangars

Gibbs
Meadow

g

gap

s

gap

s

s

s

old railway

s

s

s

garden

g

| 100 m |

N

Way Map 18: Gibbs Meadow to Kirkbride

186

The church lies on the western edge of the site of the Roman fort (dated around 120 AD) which itself lay at the western end of Stanegate. The Stanegate was a narrow military zone containing a cross-country military road complete with forts, fortlets and signal towers. This road was linked with Carlisle and Corbridge and possibly with a westwards early warning system towards Cardurnock. The Stanegate probably developed over a period of time as the Romans withdrew their troops from Scotland.

Supplies for the soldiers on this frontier were possibly shipped via the River Waver. This Trajanic fort played an important role during the second century, spanning the last years of Trajan's rule and the first part of Hadrian's.

There are some indications that the original churchyard was round, implying that pagan worship took place here in pre-Christian times. The church building is essentially Norman, though built of Roman stones with a chancel arch suggesting Saxon work. The simple construction was rescued from dereliction at the end of the nineteenth century.

As you enter the church there are recesses on either side of the doorway and it is possible that these held massive timbers to barricade the door against Scots raiders. A walled-up post-Norman 'Devil's door' can be seen. (The evil spirits were thought to flee through this door when a child was baptised.) Hanging in the chancel arch is a framed, sixteenth-century Italian plaster panel depicting the Entombment. This is believed to have come from a nineteenth-century grave. On the wall of the church is an inscription to an early vicar who kept faith through a smallpox epidemic in 1746 which claimed the lives of his wife and six children. There are also two Norman windows and an east window depicting three Irish saints: St Bride, St Patrick and St Columba.

CHAPTER 17

KIRKBRIDE
TO CARLISLE

From the gate to St Bride's Church, cross Church Road and go down an enclosed path to emerge with care on the road below. Turn right on the road, cross Whitrigg Bridge over the river Wampool and go up to the road junction where there is a choice of routes.

The River Wampool, like the Eden, can exhibit a noticeable tidal bore. The riverside fields used to be open common land. A bridleway, shown on OS maps, goes towards the Wampool a little further upstream but, as yet, there is no bridge over the river.

KIRKBRIDE TO BURGH-BY-SANDS
The Official Route
From the junction to the north of Whitrigg Bridge, turn right along the road, ignore both left turns, and continue until the river again flows adjacent to the road. Leave the road to go left down the second enclosed track (waymarked to Drumburgh). This section of the walk is shown on **Way Map 19**.

At the far end of the track go through the facing gate to enter a rough field which is part of the Cumbria Wildlife Trust Drumburgh Reserve. Go away from the left-hand boundary. Then, when almost at the far boundary, go half-left to meet an enclosed path on your left. This gives access to a track which takes you over Drumburgh Moss SSSI and into the village of Drumburgh.

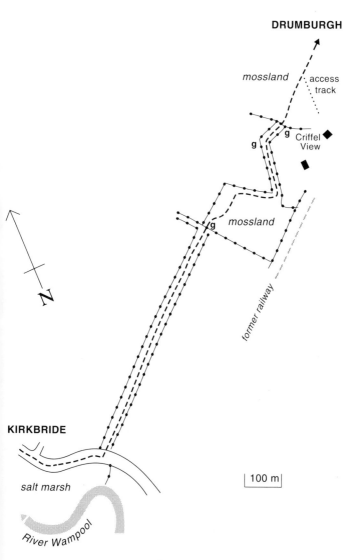

Way Map 19: Drumburgh Moss

The moss, or flow, consists of layers of decaying plants, especially sphagnum moss, which have built up some 15 m (50 ft) of peat above the deposits of boulder clay laid down during the last ice age. As in all peat mosses, controlled burning is used to keep the heather down. Under other conditions fire can wreak havoc by burning the peat, so *please* take care to avoid any danger of starting a fire. Bog rosemary, cranberry, bog asphodel, bog cotton and great sundew grow here, whilst the adder, lizard, newt, frog and toad have all been noted.

Cardurnock Peninsula Route

A second route from Kirkbride takes you round the Cardurnock Peninsula to Bowness and on to Drumburgh. This route branches left at the road junction after the crossing of the River Wampool. The peninsula would be one of the highlights of the walk, with Moricambe Bay and the Solway so close and with so much wildlife, if you didn't have to use the road. However permission to walk on the saltings has not been granted by landowners and tenants.

There is a Royal Society for the Protection of Birds reserve on the Solway at Campfield and much of historic interest in the area. The reserve occupies an 81 hectare (200 acre) farm and 6 per cent of the world's pink-foot goose population find a winter haven here. The remains of an ancient cross (most likely post-Roman) have been put behind barbed wire; the communication masts mark the site of one of three wartime airfields in the area. The others are at Silloth and Kirkbride.

The belt of saltings fringing the Solway consists of saltmarsh and slightly higher merse (land that isn't covered by the sea except at very high tides). From the estuarine silt there is a gradual transition to the sea-washed turf for which the county is famous. There are also terraces that show the changes in sea level over the centuries. It was in the badly drained patches of land that the most impressive landscape features accumulated. The formation of peat, especially at Bowness Common and Drumburgh Moss, are the best examples.

Bowness Common Route

A third route goes across the middle of Cardurnock Peninsula to the west of Bowness via Rogerscough Farm. This route (which is only suitable for competent map readers) crosses Bowness Common SSSI, but changing water levels, together with the heather and peat and navigation problems, make this a difficult option.

Bowness Common SSSI is another remnant of the once extensive peat mosses of the area and one which English Nature have a great deal of interest in. This site of some 4000 hectares (9884 acres) enables scientists to study the ecological history of the area by retaining pollen in different levels of peat laid down at different times. The area harbours much interesting plant life.

This route enables you to visit Bowness and Port Carlisle. It also crosses the Solway Junction railway line that crossed the Solway. This line was built in the 1860s as a shorter route than the one through Carlisle, mainly to serve the developing iron industries. The viaduct, from Bowness to Annan, became unsafe after winter ice got into the hollow iron supports following the branch closure in the 1920s. It was demolished in 1934–5, thus removing a dangerous pedestrian route for Scots wishing to reach the Bowness pub (in the days when Scottish pubs were closed on Sundays). For further details refer to *The Solway Junction Railway* by S. Edgar and J.M. Sinton (see Bibliography).

The Hadrian's Wall National Trail is planned to run from Bowness to Port Carlisle and on to Drumburgh. However until its route is agreed you will have to use the OS map to rejoin the main route.

Bowness-on-Solway

The Roman fort at Bowness-on-Solway is said to have been the second-largest on Hadrian's Wall and its site is now occupied by the village. This Roman fort at the end of the wall, called Mais or Maia, was started under Platorius Nepos

191

Bowness-on-Solway lies just west of the Coastal Way and marks the western end of Hadrian's Wall.

in about 127 AD and appears to have faced east along the wall. A temple to Matres was incorporated. Many buildings in the village of Bowness, including the church, contain masonry from the fort.

The Roman Wall runs almost 70 miles east from Bowness, although there is no standing wall on our route. East of Bowness raiders come by ford over the Solway or overland; west of Bowness there were no fords. However the guards still had to watch out for seaborne raids. The western third of the wall was an earth construction and, at Burgh-by-Sands, based on a cobble foundation. Only further east are there remains of the stone-built wall.

St Patrick, patron saint of Ireland, is thought to have been born at Bowness-on-Solway in 386 AD although the most celebrated saint in North Cumbria from around these times was Kentigern.

St Michael's Church, with its Norman doorway, windows

and font, has a fascinating story connected with its bells. The original church bells were stolen by the Scots but, being too heavy to carry in the chase, they were lost in the Solway. The two bells in the church porch are dated 1612 and are said to have been taken from Dornock and Middlebe in a successful revenge raid. Any new rector of Dornock has a duty to ask for the return of the bells.

On the outside wall of the former Bowness village pub is a plaque showing the layout of the Roman fort in relation to the existing settlement. It was from this village that the shortest of the Solway fords, Bowness Wath (Annan Wath to the Scots), left the shore.

Port Carlisle
Port Carlisle was built as a harbour for Carlisle but was soon replaced by Silloth. It was linked to the city by canal in 1823, even though the original intention had been to build the canal to Maryport. Later, in 1854, the canal bed became a railway line, and a piece of the old rolling stock can be seen in the National Railway Museum in York. Had other, more ambitious plans for the canal been executed (the original proposal was to build it across the Pennines to Newcastle), the history of this settlement might have been very different.

As it was, people could reach Port Carlisle by sea from Liverpool in a day and then boats would be towed along, in an hour and forty minutes, to Carlisle. The canal never paid its way but the Carlisle manufacturers were the directors and they were happy to receive cheap freightage rather than dividends.

The fate of Port Carlisle was finally sealed when the Solway Junction Railway was built in 1869. For fifty years, until 1914, the railway was operated by a horse-drawn Dandy carriage. Steam trains then ran to Port Carlisle until 1932.

The original settlement here was called Fishers Cross. However this site was not the earliest port of Carlisle. That was Sandsfield, near Burgh-by-Sands. There is some fine Georgian architecture in Port Carlisle, which is a Conservation Area, and many of the houses are listed buildings.

Drumburgh

Drumburgh (pronounced Drumbruff) is on both the Solway and Hadrian's Wall. Little remains of the Wall between here and Carlisle but there are telltale signs of its line and of the adjacent *vallum* (ditch).

Drumburgh Castle is now a house but was rebuilt in 1558 by Lord Dacre to replace a pele tower of 1307 erected with stones taken from Hadrian's Wall. Thomas Leland described it as a 'pretty pyle for defns of the contery'. Like other border strongholds, it played a crucial role in repulsing Scottish raids. In this case the problem arose from the relative ease with which the reivers could cross the Solway at low tides. The house was completely repaired in 1681 and is probably the model for 'Whiteladies' in Sir Walter Scott's *Redgauntlet*. A whitewashed Roman altar stands on the steps.

To the north-west of the castle is a smaller tower which might have been an eighteenth-century lookout point. Drumburgh possibly marked the end of the Sandwath ford.

Turn right on the road and continue along the verge, with the River Eden channel across the saltings to your left. On this long, straight stretch you pass below Boustead Hill before arriving at the end of the marsh. The official Way continues along the road into Burgh-by-Sands (pronounced Bruff). The Hadrian's Wall Trail, when it is finalised, should enhance the route by improving the foot path surface off the road.

Before entering Burgh-by-Sands the road crosses the edge of Burgh Marsh. Such marshes are used for overwintering Lakeland fell sheep, the climate here being somewhat milder than on high fellsides. Usually the farmers send hoggs (younger sheep, possibly in their first winter) and this enables the poorer grazing in the fell areas to sustain larger flocks.

Burgh Marsh, noted for its mushrooms, is an area of common land. Horse-racing took place here regularly until 1900. The most fiercely contested races were for the Barony Cups which were awarded, from 1690, when a new Earl of

Lonsdale assumed the title. There were six of these cups. Robert Anderson's ballad 'Burgh Races in 1804' says: 'The cup was aw siller, and letter'd reet neycely'. A National Hunt programme ran here from 1882 to 1900.

Burgh-by-Sands

It was here at Burgh that the Roman fort Aballava stood astride Hadrian's Wall, its exact site lying beneath the present-day village. The fort, built under Nepos in 122–126 AD, covered some 20 hectares (49 acres) and offered its devotions to the Roman god Hercules. The site of a further Roman fort was found to the south of the village in the 1980s.

Like Newton Arlosh, Burgh Church has a heavily fortified pele tower constructed from Roman masonry. The fourteenth-century tower was entered by a small door in a large iron frame. The dark east end, without a window, also had a tower and was perhaps the priest's residence. Edward I lay in state here and one of the south side windows depicts him. There are few such 'baste towers' left in this part of the world, Newton Arlosh, Brackenrigg, Glasson and Burgh being the only ones recorded. There used to be one at Bowness; the one at Drumburgh is a replica of an earlier structure.

Lamonby Farm, Burgh, is a clay daubin (or dobbin) construction. Although these structures were usually occupied by poorer people this one is rather more elaborate than most. Due to the lack of other suitable materials, clay was quite frequently used for building on the Solway Plain. The thatched roof is held by a cruck frame, a feature that can be noted in other parts of the village. Originally, half of the thatch and mud construction was reserved for animals and half for humans. Though cheap to build, these dwellings deteriorate rapidly.

BURGH-BY-SANDS TO CARLISLE

From Burgh to Carlisle the Way shares the same route as the proposed Hadrian's Wall National Trail. However an alternative route keeps closer to the coast and riverbank and visits the King Edward I memorial on Burgh Marsh. This alternative is not suitable at very high tides or when the Eden carries a lot of floodwater. Use the OS map to follow the riverbank route from Burgh to Beaumont, and from east of Kirkandrews to Grinsdale.

A small circular diversion from Burgh enables you to visit the monument to King Edward I on Burgh Marsh. It was here that Edward, the 'hammer of the Scots', died in his tent in 1307, aged 68. Based at Holme Cultram, he came here in order to crush the Scots. He launched his campaign in response to Robert the Bruce's rebellion and subsequent coronation at Scone in 1306. It was from this site that Edward's army crossed the Solway fords. The monument, supposedly marking the site of his death tent, was built in 1685 by the Duke of Norfolk. It fell down in 1795 and was rebuilt on several occasions. Contrary to his wishes, Edward was buried in Westminster Abbey.

Sandsfield
From the monument follow the saltings north, keeping near the field boundary, to Old Sandsfield. Haaf netting fishermen can sometimes be seen in the waters using the fishing technique possibly introduced by the Vikings, whereby the tide flows through nets held by rigid poles. In the twelfth century a fishery at Sandsfield, consisting of one net, was granted to the monks of Holme Cultram. This was followed, in 1234, by permission to build a house. Later Sandsfield became Carlisle's original port and possibly served as a munitions port for Edward I in the fourteenth century. There was also a toll station for the Scots, as Sandsfield is adjacent to a ford.

It continued as a port until the late eighteenth century and, like other Solway ports, suffered from the major storm of 1796. Until then ships of up to 80 tonnes could reach this part of the River Eden and imports far exceeded exports. The major incoming commodities were timber, iron, flax, tar, rice and mercantile goods, whilst wheat, butter and alabaster

This monument on Burgh Marsh marks the place where Edward I died in 1307.

made up the bulk of the small exports. Needless to say, such a location – on the misty marshlands of the border – had a reputation as a smugglers' haunt.

Old Sandsfield was probably the site of the Peatwath crossing where, in 1216, a couple of thousand Scottish soldiers were drowned after retreating from a raid on Holme Cultram Abbey. New Sandsfield is the likely location of another ford, the Stonewath, and this part of the river is a good place to see the tidal bore.

Take the Carlisle road out of Burgh and go over Hallstones Bridge beyond the village sign. About 50 m (55 yds) further, on the left, you will see a gated track next to an iron stile. Cross this stile and follow the left-hand boundary to a stiled footbridge which you cross. In the next field go towards the line of trees. Follow them and the subsequent avenue to reach a stile. Over the stile, follow the enclosed lane and track, on the line of Hadrian's Wall, all the way into Beaumont. Turn right on to the road and then left at the green below the church.

Beaumont

Beaumont (pronounced Beemont) means 'beautiful hill', a hill occupied by St Mary's Church. The village is situated on top of a wooded bluff above the Eden that was once the site of a Roman mile castle.

The church was originally built by the Normans and incorporates Roman masonry. Despite the fact that two nineteenth-century restorations have greatly altered St Mary's it still retains the simplicity of a dales chapel. The walled-in east end has three small windows and the chain on the font cover is weighted with a lead dove. Two of the ancient stones are in the west end. The nearby ford over the Eden was used by the Scots to avoid the Carlisle garrison, the river here being relatively narrow.

Follow the signposted Cumbria Coastal Way route left from the green down the cul-de-sac, by the telephone box.

When the road turns left, go through the small gate on your right and follow the path down through the wooded bluff called The Heugh. After a bridge the path follows the riverbank. It then climbs some steps to the top of the bluff and goes left on to the line of Hadrian's Wall. Pass over a stile, go below the house and cross a further stile, with a footpath sign where the riverbank route to Grinsdale departs.

Continue along the right-hand fence to cross a further stile by a wooden hut. Go along the edge of the wood, turn right at the far end of the tennis courts, then left through the gate in the corner. Follow the right-hand boundary to a further gate and emerge on the road. Go left, through Kirkandrews, and left again on the main road (signed to Carlisle).

Kirkandrews-on-Eden parish is amalgamated with Beaumont; its own parish church, which gives the village its name, was closed in 1692. The churchyard is still used as a burial ground and corresponds with the site of a Roman mile castle on Hadrian's Wall. Until about 1800 the burial services were apparently read under the shattered chancel arch (now no longer standing). St Andrew's well is situated below the graveyard.

When the pavement ends go left down the track and keep right at the junction. Just beyond the junction turn right over the stile and gradually climb the bank in the field to your right. Walk along the top of the bank until the hedgerow gives way to a wire fence.

Cross the stile behind the tree on your right. Then turn left and follow the left-hand fence along the top of the embankment to cross a further stile in the far left-hand field corner.

Follow the right-hand hedge to cross a stiled footbridge, Sourmilk Bridge, and continue to the gate in the far right-hand corner of the next field. Through this gate, follow the track ahead, through the copse, and into Grinsdale via the yard of Park Farm.

Grinsdale

Grinsdale is a hamlet with some eighteenth-century buildings and it has an unusually situated church overlooking the River Eden on a wooded bluff. To reach it from the village, you have to take the path after the last house on the right (called Sunnybank) and cross two fields. Only brides and, one presumes, the departed, are permitted to go by car to the church. It is one of several Cumbrian churches dedicated to St Kentigern, a dedication unique to Cumbria. This saint also features in stained glass windows in both Bowness and Burgh Churches. He ministered in this part of the world when it was part of Scotland and he was symbolically associated with the robin and the salmon. St Kentigern, also known as St Mungo, is patron saint of Glasgow.

The original church was served by a monk from Lanercost Priory until the Dissolution when this arrangement ceased and the church fell into ruin. It was rebuilt in 1740 and services restarted the following year. The church was restored again in 1895. It is the beautiful churchyard and the church's scenic setting, which make it worth visiting but it also has its place in history. On 10th November 1745 a contingent of Bonnie Prince Charles's army crossed the Eden below this church on their way to capture Carlisle.

Turn right on the road through Grinsdale village and, just after the last building on the left, turn off the road over a stile. Take the footpath (signed to the River Eden) and go directly ahead to cross the footbridge. Go to the right in the field, then left after 20 m (22 yds). Follow the left-hand trees, slowly rising into a wooded bluff, and cross a stile in the far-left hand corner of the field.

Follow the path along the top of the bluff, descend to the footbridge, and climb back to a stile to re-enter a field. Continue along the left-hand boundary, with the Eden below. Descend to a further footbridge and climb a little way to cross another stile.

In the next field continue above the river to a stile in the left-hand corner. Go over the stile and continue until you are opposite the last pylon in the field. Drop down to cross a footbridge and climb the steps, then follow the left-hand fence through rough ground, formerly a railway siding. Descend the steps at the end to go under a former railway bridge over the Eden.

Into Carlisle

From here to Carlisle centre, follow the riverbank path as it goes under the railway and meanders round the Sheepmount Recreation Ground, to the River Caldew just next to its confluence with the Eden. Cross this bridge and continue straight ahead, ignoring the access road to the right. Follow the tree-lined avenue, with the castle over to your right, as you pass through Bitts Park and on to Eden Bridge with the Sands Leisure Centre beyond.

CHAPTER 18

CARLISLE AND ON TO GRETNA

CARLISLE

Carlisle is a fine northern city with a chequered history, owing to its location on the English/Scottish border. Of all English cities it has probably seen the most military action. Famous occupants, such as William Rufus and Mary Queen of Scots, and prisoners, such as Kinmont Willie, have added to the local folklore.

The original city stood on the earth section of the Hadrian's Wall. In 79 AD Agricola built the first fort, Luguvalium, here, using turf and timber. A later replacement was built in stone and continued in military use until around 320 AD. Just north-east of the city centre lay the large fort of Stanwix, Ala Petriona, which housed around 1000 soldiers.

The city fluctuated between English and Scottish control for several centuries. During the tenth century a treaty was signed that incorporated much of north-west Cumbria into Scotland. The Normans did not reach the area until 1092, when William Rufus completed the conquest. Hence this part of England is missing from the *Domesday Book*.

The city walls were constructed in the twelfth century, in the reign of Henry I. David I of Scotland then wrested Carlisle back for the Scots during the civil war following Henry I's death. He took the border down to the Duddon, heightened the city walls and built the castle keep. Henry II later gained the city back for England, although the bishops of Glasgow still claimed some of the area as part of their diocese until the thirteenth century.

The bloody conflict continued into the sixteenth century when the raids carried out by the reivers were at their height. Cattle-thieving took place between families on both sides of the border and tension was increased by inter-family feuds and opposition to law-keepers. G. MacDonald Fraser gives a full account of the border troubles in *The Steel Bonnets* (see Bibliography).

In the English Civil War the city was a Royalist stronghold and was besieged for nine months, during which time the citizens were reduced to eating horses and rats.

In the seventeenth and eighteenth centuries Carlisle was a base for successful woollen and cotton manufacturing. The nineteenth century saw it become a major railway centre.

Carlisle Castle

Carlisle Castle was begun in 1092 when William Rufus built a palisade on the hill after he had seized the city, but it was the Scottish King David I who actually laid out the castle with a tower and ditches. In the sixteenth century Elizabeth I was responsible for many of the repairs and her cousin Mary Queen of Scots was imprisoned here in 1568. During its history the castle has served as a fortress and, for a short time during the border troubles, as a royal palace for Edward I.

The massive sandstone ramparts of Carlisle Castle.

A Roman altar stone, to Jupiter, was removed from de Ireby's Tower in the 1980s and is now on display. The tower itself incorporates stone from an earlier tower. The soft sandstone rock enabled prisoners to make engravings in their cell walls and these, dating from around 1480, can still be seen in the keep. Besides the castle (which charges for admission), there is also the Border Regiment Museum (open all year round), housed in Queen Mary's Tower.

> From outside the castle go under the road using the subway.

Tullie House

On the right you will see the entrance to Tullie House (Carlisle Museum and Art Gallery). A visit to this superb museum, newly extended and reopened in 1991, is essential for a complete understanding of much of the countryside through which we have passed. The original Jacobean building is part of the complex and is itself built over a Roman site. The museum is open all year round and includes displays on the Romans, the reivers, the siege of Carlisle, and Cumbrian wildlife.

> After your visit to the museum, which can easily take up a good few hours, leave by the gardens in the south-west corner and turn left into Abbey Street. Pass the Abbey gateway to view an imposing section of the city walls, then return to Prior Slee's gateway.
>
> Through here, enter the cathedral precinct and go past the Old Registry (dated 1699) and the front of the Deanery. Permission to visit this latter building, with its remarkable ceiling of painted panels, can be sought in the cathedral.

Carlisle Cathedral

Carlisle Cathedral was once a monastery. Although its stones were used to strengthen the castle during times of strife, the building still retains some of its original Norman fabric. An Augustinian priory was established here in 1133 and completed in 1419. After the dissolution of the priory in 1540 the cathedral church was re-dedicated. In 1645 there was further demolition to add to the city fortifications.

Although it is one of England's smallest cathedrals, Carlisle has seen its share of history. Here Edward I excommunicated Robert the Bruce with 'bell, book and candle.' The cathedral has a fourteenth-century east window, claimed as the finest in Europe, and carved and canopied choir stalls, complete with misericords dating back to 1400. The Prior's Tower, which can be visited, is a fifteenth-century pele tower. There is also the Cathedral Treasury Museum (open all year from about 10 a.m. to 5 p.m., admission free), which displays Viking, Celtic and early Christian artefacts, bishops' copes and historic church plate.

A Walk Round Carlisle
Leave the cathedral precinct by the south-west exit and go to the city walls and Sally Port.

This gateway was used by Royalist soldiers when they raided the Roundhead army during the civil war. Earlier it may have been a place where goods were delivered to the medieval tithe barn (the tithe being a tenth of each person's income, usually rendered to the Church in the form of goods or grain).

Across the road go left to St Cuthbert's Church. St Cuthbert's Church was built in 1778 and is named after the Bishop of Carlisle from 686 AD. Indeed there has been a church on this site ever since the saint's visit. The pulpit (dated 1905) is mounted on rails, and is moved into the centre of the aisle when the sermon is due to be given.

From St Cuthbert's Church go to the Market Square where the Guildhall lies on your left.

This building (dated 1407) now houses a museum which displays the city's stocks and pillories, along with antiquities from various trade guilds. (Opening hours are 11 a.m. to 4 p.m. on Tuesday–Saturday and Bank Holidays; 12 to 5 p.m.

on Sunday, admission free.) The house is timber framed, and painted figures on the eaves are said to ward off bad luck.

Just beyond is the old town hall, market cross and square. The old town hall is now the tourist information centre. The market cross was erected in 1682 on the site of the Roman forum, and public proclamations are still made from its steps.

> Continue down English Street, past the Citadel, at the edge of the city walls.

Just beyond is the railway station. The Citadel, originally built as a fort by Henry VIII in 1541, was the southern gateway into the city. It last saw action in 1745 when its cannons were used by the Scots against the Duke of Cumberland's forces. It was rebuilt in 1810 to become the city's courthouse. Notice the old toll board where people were charged for the right to bring goods into Carlisle.

This last stage takes us on to the land of the real Solway, for our walk now runs near the original Sulwath which, as mentioned earlier, may have given rise to the Solway name. In many ways the walk from Carlisle to Rockcliffe is like the Sandsfield to Carlisle route in reverse. The River Eden is always a centre of interest for birdlife.

ON TO GRETNA

> Go back to the castle and the bridge over the Eden, near the Sands Leisure Centre. Cross the Eden by the main road bridge and on the far bank go left down a path adjacent to the cricket ground entrance. Bear left above the ski slope and walk down to Hyssop Holme Well. Continue straight ahead, then via the riverbank, until you eventually climb to the road, Etterby Scaur. Follow the pavement left and take the first left-hand turning in front of the Redfern pub. Etterby Road leads you to Carlisle Youth Hostel (up for sale at the time of writing).
>
> Just beyond the hostel go left down the signed track, where Stainton Road bends right. Go down the track, via a gate and kissing gate, to follow the river embankment path.

Go under the right-hand side of the former railway bridge and continue along the embankment through long, narrow fields. Continue parallel to the river to pass under the overhead wires.

The path and river bear right, via a series of stiles, opposite Grinsdale, where its isolated church can best be seen. Continue along the path, hugging the river meander, before climbing, via another stile, to the landward side of a small wooded bluff by the left-hand fence. Go over a further stile and footbridge, descending to the riverbank.

At very high water, especially in flood, this stretch can be waterlogged. This is especially so around Rockcliffe.

From here the path virtually follows the riverbank all the way to Rockcliffe. However you need to keep next to the right-hand boundary of the saltings and the enclosed land to pass a section of river, just short of Rockcliffe, which has an island. A whole series of stiles, the odd footbridge, small fisherfolks' car parks and a fishing hut are passed.

Cargo

The route goes near the village of Cargo which is an amalgam of old and new houses almost all along the main street. The only real excuse for leaving the riverbank path is to visit the Four Oaks pub which serves meals. This is partially hidden, off to the left of the main street. The wath at Cargo was one of the routes taken by Bonnie Prince Charlie's army in 1745 before they regrouped to attack Carlisle. They also used fords at Grinsdale and Rockcliffe.

Over the footbridge, just below Rockcliffe church, bear right on the saltings to reach the road.

Rockcliffe

Here, as in a few other places, the River Eden has cut small, red sandstone cliffs. Go to the road adjacent to the houses. Rockcliffe church, dedicated to St Mary, was built in 1848 but the churchyard contains a fine fragment of an ancient cross with a solid wheel head and dragon decoration. You will have to pass the church if you want to get a meal at the Crown and Thistle pub.

> Follow the road to your left, away from the church, to climb over the riverbank cliffs. Continue until the road bends to the right by some farm buildings. Go down a track, by a stile and gate, to the riverbank on your left. Keep near the right-hand boundary of the saltings to reach, via a gate, Demesne Farm.

Near the riverbank you pass Castletown House which merited inclusion in Pevsner's Buildings of England series. He described the house, built in 1831, as 'a fine ashlar faced Grecian House' with 'a good interior'. Private visits can be arranged by telephoning 0228–74205 in advance.

To our west lies Rockcliffe Marsh, a huge area of saltings that did not exist in the fourteenth century and which owes its existence to the constantly changing coastline. Now the marsh has a sea defence wall. In winter, pink-foot and barnacle geese gather here to graze the turf.

> Turn right to go through the farmyard. Then use the farm access road and take the first right turn to reach a T-junction. Go left on this next road and enter the field on your right by a stile (with footpath sign). Go along the left-hand boundary of the field, cross the stile in the corner and go left by the left-hand boundary of the wood. Go towards Wether Hill Farm and turn right through the red gate by the house. Go through the farmyard to the road.
>
> Go left on the road. After the next farm on the right, Halltown Farm, as the road bends left, cross the stile by the footpath sign on your right. Follow the right-hand fence and cross a stile and track. Continue in the same direction, parallel to the yard, to cross a stile and footbridge. Go left in the wooded area, and cross a stile. Follow the left-hand hedge to cross a further stile and gain an enclosed lane.
>
> Go down to Garriestown Farm, pass through the yard by a gate and continue down the farm access road until it bends right. Here go through the gate and stile on your left,

follow the enclosed track and then the railway line. The path now goes along the bank of the Esk. To reach Metal Bridge Inn go over the stile on your right to the pub car park.

Metal Bridge

Metal Bridge Inn serves food. Its name derives from the earliest bridge designed by the Scottish engineer Thomas Telford and erected in 1815. There is still a plaque but Cumberland County Council replaced the bridge in 1920 with a concrete one. This bridge now carries the A74 over the River Esk, just next to the inn.

The River Esk is in many ways a watershed. Until 1552, it marked the boundary with Scotland. The area between here and the River Sark, the current national boundary, was referred to as 'The Debatable Land', despite the fact it was not claimed by England until the fifteenth century. This region was extremely lawless during the time of the border reivers. Today the main activity is the extraction of peat from the Solway Moss, the site of a battle in 1542.

The Sulwath

The Sulwath was a ford over the River Esk. It was also a meeting place where border law was enforced. Its exact position is somewhat uncertain, due to the changing areas of saltings. Esk Boathouse, 1.6 km (1 mile) downstream from Metal Bridge, is one possible location, as is the famous Lochmaben Stone to the south-west of Gretna. Certainly the stone was a site where border wardens met to seek redress.

You can get a bus back from Metal Bridge to Carlisle if you wish. (The bus shelter is on the southbound side of the A74 – see Useful Addresses and Information for the relevant bus numbers.) However the purists have to make their way a further 3 km (2 miles) by the A74 to the River Sark and into Scotland. The route lies mostly alongside the A74 but the old road goes off left to Sark Bridge, thus sparing you the noise of the traffic. The embankment round the edge of the marsh does not have a right of way, as its use could interfere with wildlife in this part of the Solway SSSI.

Useful Addresses and Information

Albright and Wilson (Marchon Works),
PO Box 15, Whitehaven CA28 9QQ
Tel: 0946 693131

Allerdale District Council (Planning Department and
Tourism Section),
Allerdale House, Workington CA14 3YJ
Tel: 0900 604351

Barrow-in-Furness Borough Council (Tourism and Planning
Departments),
Town Hall, Duke Street, Barrow-in-Furness LA14 2LD
Tel: 0229 825500

BBC
Local radio wavelengths:
South Cumbria 96.1 VHF; 358m Medium Wave
North Cumbria 95.6 VHF; 397m Medium Wave

British Gas, Barrow Shore Terminal,
Rampside, Barrow-in-Furness LA13 0QS
Tel: 0229 838811

British Nuclear Fuels Ltd,
Sellafield Works, Seascale CA20 1PG
Tel: 09467 28333

Carlisle City Council (Countryside Officer),
Civic Centre, Rickergate, Carlisle CA3 8QG
Tel: 0228 23411

Copeland Borough Council (Planning and Tourism Sections),
Civic Hall, Lowther Street, Whitehaven CA28 7SH
Tel: 0946 693111

Cumbria County Council,
The Courts, Carlisle CA3 8NA
Tel: 0228 23456

Cumbria Wildlife Trust,
The Badger's Paw, Church Street, Ambleside LA22 0BU
Tel: 05395 32476

Ectona Fibres Ltd,
Siddick, Workington CA14 11LG
Tel: 0900 603651

English Nature,
Blackwell,
Bowness-on-Windermere LA23 3JR
Tel: 05394 45286

Flying Buzzard,
Maryport Harbour, Maryport
Tel: 0900 815954

Friends of the Lake District,
Number 3, Yard 77, Highgate, Kendal LA9 4ED
Tel: 0539 720788

Helena Thompson Museum,
Park End Road, Workington CA14 4DE
Tel: 0900 602598

Lake District Planning Board (Park Management Service),
Murley Moss,
Oxenholme Rd,
Kendal LA9 7RL
Tel: 0539 724555

Ray Porter,
Guide to the Leven Sands,
Tel: 0229 580935

LOCAL PAPERS

Most newspapers include tide times.
Barrow Evening Mail (Mon–Sat)
Cumberland News (Fri)
West Cumberland Times and Star (Fri)
Westmorland Gazette (Fri)
Whitehaven News (Thur)
There are also one or two freebies, such as the *West Cumbrian Gazette*.

Maryport Maritime Museum and Tourist Information Centre,
1 Senhouse Street, Maryport CA15 6AB
Tel: 0900 813738

Millom Folk Museum and Tourist Information Centre,
St George's Road, Millom LA18 4DD
Tel: 0229 772555

Cedric Robinson (Queen's Guide to the Kent Sands),
Guides Farm, Cart Lane,
Kents Bank, Grange-over-Sands LA11 7AF
Tel: 05395 32165

Senhouse Roman Museum,
The Battery, Maryport CA15 6JD
Tel: 0900 816168

South Lakeland Council (Tourism Department and Footpath
Sections),
South Lakeland House, Lowther Street, Kendal LA9 4QQ
Tel: 0539 733333

South Walney Nature Reserve,
The Warden, South Walney Nature Reserve, Barrow-in-
Furness LA14 3YQ
Tel: 0229 471066

TOURIST INFORMATION CENTRES

Barrow-in-Furness Forum 28, Duke Street, Barrow LA14
1HU. Tel: 0229 870156
Carlisle The Old Town Hall, Carlisle CA3 8JH. Tel: 0228
512444
Grange-over-Sands Victoria Hall, Main Street, Grange LA11
6PT. Tel: 05395 34026
Maryport Maritime Museum, 1 Senhouse Street, Maryport
CA15 6AB. Tel 0900 813738
Millom Folk Museum, George's Road, Millom LA18 4DQ.
Tel: 0229 772555
Ravenglass La'al Ratty Car Park (Seasonal) CA18 1SW.
Tel: 0229 717278
Silloth The Green, Silloth CA5 4QP. Tel: 06973 31944
Ulverston Coronation Hall, County Square, Ulverston, LA12
7LZ. Tel: 0229 587120

Whitehaven Market Hall, Market Place, Whitehaven CA28
7JG. Tel: 0946 695678
Workington Central Car Park, Washington Street,
Workington CA14 3AW. Tel: 0900 602923

VSEL,
Barrow-in-Furness LA14 1AF
Tel: 0229 823366

Whitehaven Museum and Art Gallery,
Civic Hall, Lowther Street, Whitehaven CA28 7SH
Tel: 0946 693111

Workington Hall (Curwen Hall),
Curwen Park, Workington CA14 4AW
Contact via Allerdale Tourism Dept. or Workington Tourist
Information Centre (see above).

BUS SERVICES

Tel: 0946 63222 for all Cumberland Motor Services (CMS)
buses to check days and times of operation. Check details of
other buses at local tourist information centres or by
telephoning Cumbria Connections on 0228 812812.

5 Whitehaven – Bransty – Parton – Lowca (CMS)
6 Ulverston – Barrow (CMS)
6 and 12 Whitehaven – Egremont – Seascale (CMS)
11 Ulverston – Coast Road – Barrow (CMS)
12 Seascale – Whitehaven (CMS)
13 Holmrook – Millom (William Sim & Son)
15 Millom – Haverigg – Millom (CMS)
16 Eskmeals – Bootle – Millom (CMS)
20 Whitehaven – St Bees (CMS)
30 Maryport – Workington – Whitehaven (CMS)
34 Whitehaven – Workington (CMS)
38/38A Carlisle – Wigton – Silloth (CMS)
40 Skinburness – Maryport (Carr Coaches)
40, 1 Allonby – Silloth (Carr Coaches)
41 Silloth – Kirkbride – Bowness-on-Solway (Carr Coaches)
43 Silloth – Abbeytown (J. W. Messenger & Son)
48 Workington – Harrington (CMS)
71 Carlisle – Anthorn – Silloth (CMS)

79 Carlisle – Gretna (CMS and Western Scottish)
82 Carlisle – Gretna (Western Scottish)
93 Carlisle – Burgh-by-Sands – Bowness-on-Solway (CMS)
98 Carlisle – Gretna (CMS)
101 Carlisle – Cargo – Rockcliffe – Gretna (CMS)
110 Carlisle – Gretna (MacEwans Coaches)
254 Lancaster – Carnforth – Silverdale (Ribble)
300 Whitehaven – Workington – Maryport – Aspatria –
   Wigton – Carlisle (CMS)
503 Newbiggin – Baycliffe (CMS)
509 Ulverston – Kirkby-in-Furness (CMS)
518 Haverthwaite – Ulverston (CMS)
530 Grange – Flookburgh – Cark and Milnthorpe – Levens
   Bridge (CMS)
535 Cartmel – Haverthwaite – Ulverston (CMS)
552 Arnside – Milnthorpe – Levens Bridge (CMS)
810 Millom – Bootle – Ravenglass – Seascale (Hodgsons)
812 Barrow – Foxfield – Millom (Hodgsons)
830 Nethertown – St Bees (S. H. Brownrigg)
834 St Bees – Whitehaven (S. H. Brownrigg)
911 Silloth – Bowness – Wigton (CMS)
912 Workington – Silloth – Skinburness (CMS)
X5 Sellafield – Whitehaven – Harrington – Workington
   (CMS)

TRAIN SERVICES
British Rail
Barrow Station: 0229 820805
Whitehaven Station: 0946 692414
Workington Station: 0900 602575
Carlisle Station: 0228 44711
Coastal Way stations on the Carlisle – Workington – Barrow –
Lancaster line: Silverdale (Lancashire); Arnside; Grange;
Kents Bank; Cark; Ulverston; Roose; Barrow; Askam;
Kirkby-in-Furness; Foxfield; Green Road; Millom; Silecroft;
Bootle; Ravenglass; Drigg; Seascale; Sellafield; Baystones;
Nethertown; St Bees; Whitehaven (Bransty); Parton;
Harrington; Workington; Flimby; Maryport and Carlisle.

Ravenglass and Eskdale Railway
Tel: 0229 717171

ACCOMMODATION AND FACILITIES

The following charts show availability of accommodation, food and shops along the Cumbria Coastal Way.

SECTION ONE

	Bed & Breakfast	Pub or Food	Cafe	Shop (s)	
Barrow	✔	✔	✔	✔	
Piel Island/Roa	✔	✔		✔	
Bardsea	✔	✔			
Ulverston	✔	✔	✔	✔	
Greenodd		✔		✔	
Cark		✔		✔	
Grange-over-Sands	✔	✔	✔	✔	
Gilpin Bridge	✔	✔	✔		
Milnthorpe		✔	✔	✔	
Sandside	✔	✔	✔		
Arnside	✔	✔	✔	✔	(+YHA)

SECTION TWO

	Bed & Breakfast	Pub or Food	Cafe	Shop (s)	
Silecroft	✔	✔			
Haverigg	✔	✔		✔	
Millom	✔	✔	✔	✔	
Broughton-in-Furness	✔	✔	✔	✔	
Foxfield	✔	✔			
Kirkby-in-Furness		✔		✔	
Askam-in-Furness		✔		✔	

SECTION THREE

	Bed & Breakfast	Pub or Food	Cafe	Shop (s)	
Seascale	✔	✔		✔	
Drigg		✔			
Ravenglass	✔	✔	✔	✔	

SECTION FOUR

	Bed & Breakfast	Pub or Food	Cafe	Shop (s)	
Maryport	✔	✔	✔	✔	
Flimby		✔			
Workington	✔	✔	✔	✔	
Harrington		✔		✔	
Parton		✔		✔	
Whitehaven	✔	✔	✔	✔	
St Bees	✔	✔	✔	✔	
Nethertown		✔			

SECTION FIVE

	Bed & Breakfast	Pub or Food	Cafe	Shop (s)	
Gretna	✔	✔	✔	✔	
Rockcliffe		✔			
Cargo		✔			
Carlisle	✔	✔	✔	✔	(+YHA)
Burgh-by-Sands	✔	✔		✔	
Kirkbride	✔	✔			
Newton Arlosh		✔			
Abbeytown		✔			
Skinburness	✔	✔			
Silloth	✔	✔	✔	✔	
Allonby	✔	✔	✔	✔	

BIBLIOGRAPHY

Please note that those books labelled 'o.p.' are out of print and some are very rare.

Baddeley, M.J.B., *The English Lake District,* Dulau, London, 1895 (o.p.)

Baines, *History of the County of Lancashire,* Wales, Liverpool, 1824 (o.p.)

Baldwin, J.R. & Whyte, I.D. (eds), *The Scandinavians in Cumbria,* Scottish Society for Northern Studies, Edinburgh, 1985

Banks, A.G., *H.W. Schneider of Barrow and Bowness,* Titus Wilson, Kendal, 1984

Barnes, F., *Barrow and District,* Barrow-in-Furness Borough Council, 1979

Barrow-in-Furness Borough Council, *Heritage Trails,* Barrow-in-Furness Borough Council (o.p.); *The Natural Environment of North Walney and Sandscale Haws,* Barrow-in-Furness Borough Council, 1978 (o.p.)

Bellhouse, R.L., *Roman Sites on the Cumberland Coast,* Cumberland & Westmorland Antiquarian and Archaeological Society, Kendal, 1989

Blake, B., *The Solway Firth,* Robert Hale, London, 1974 (o.p.)

Bradley, A.G., *Highways and Byways in the Lake District,* Macmillan, London, 1930 (o.p.)

Carruthers, F.J., *People Called CUMBRI,* Robert Hale, London, 1979

Clare, Tom, *Archaeological Sites of the Lake District,* Moorland Publishing, Ashbourne, 1981

Collingwood, W.G., *The Lake Counties,* J.M. Dent, London, 1932; revised by William Rollinson, J.M. Dent, London, 1988

Conishead Priory, *Official Guide,* Ulverston (o.p.)

Cumberland & Westmorland Antiquarian and Archaeological Society, *Transactions,* Various Volumes, CWAAS

Cumberland County Council, *North Cumberland Coast,* Cumberland County Council, Carlisle, undated (o.p.)

'Cumbria', *Arnside and Silverdale*, Dalesman, Clapham, 1967 (o.p.)

Edgar, S. & Sinton, J.M., *The Solway Junction Railway*, Oakwood, Wallingford, 1990

Fell, Alfred, *The Early Iron Industry of Furness and District*, Hume Kitchen, 1908 (o.p.)

Ferguson, R.S., *A History of Cumberland*, Elliot Stock, London, 1890; republished by S.R. Publishers, Wakefield, 1970 (o.p.)

Fraser, M., *Companion Into Lakeland*, Methuen, London, 1939 (o.p.)

Fraser, G. MacDonald, *The Steel Bonnets*, Pan, London, 1974 (o.p.); since republished

Hindle, Paul, *Roads and Trackways of the Lake District*, Moorland Publishing, Ashbourne, 1984

Holker Hall and Gardens: Official Guide, Holker Estate, Stafford, 1990

Johnson, S., *Hadrian's Wall*, Batsford/English Heritage, London, 1989

Knapp-Fisher, H.C., *Furness and Cartmel*, St Catherine Press, London, 1948 (o.p.)

Leach, Alice, *Furness Abbey*, Furness Heritage Press, Ulverston, 1988 (o.p.)

Linton, E. Lynn, *The Lake Country*, South-Elder, London, 1864 (o.p.)

Marshall, J.D. & Davies-Shiel, M., *Industrial Archaeology of the Lake Counties*, Michael Moon, Beckermet, 1977 (o.p.)

Millward, Roy & Robinson, Adrian, *Cumbria*, Macmillan, London, 1972 (o.p.)

Neilson, G., *Annals of the Solway Until A.D. 1307*, Glasgow Archaeological Society, 1856 (o.p.); republished by Michael Moon, Beckermet, 1974 (o.p.)

NERC/IGS, *British Regional Geology – Northern England*, HMSO, London, 1971

Nicholson, Norman, *Greater Lakeland*, Robert Hale, London, 1969 (o.p.); *Selected Poems 1940–1982*, Faber & Faber, London

Palmer, William, *The Verge of Western Lakeland*, Robert Hale, London, 1941 (o.p.)

Parker, John, *Cumbria*, Bartholomew, Edinburgh, 1977 (o.p.)

Pevsner, Nikolaus, *Buildings of England* series, North Lancashire (1969), Cumberland and Westmorland (1973), Penguin, Harmondsworth

Robinson, Cedric, *One Man's Morecambe Bay*, Dalesman, Clapham, 1984

Robinson, Cedric & Mitchell, Bill, *Life Around Morecambe Bay*, Dalesman, Clapham, 1986

Robinson, Huberta, *Walney Past and Present*, Archaeological Associates, Abermeurig, undated (o.p.)

Rollinson, William, *A History of Man in the Lake District*, J.M. Dent, London, 1967 (o.p.)

Rollinson, William (ed.), *The Lake District Landscape Heritage*, David & Charles, Newton Abbot, 1989

St Bride's Parish Church, Kirkbride, *1189–1989 Octocentenary Brochure*, Kirkbride Parish, Kirkbride, 1989 (o.p.)

Scott, Sir Walter, *Redgauntlet*, Everyman, London, 1906

Soil Survey of England & Wales, *Sheet 1 Northern England*, Soil Survey of England & Wales, HMSO, London

Smith, Kenneth, *Cumbrian Villages*, Robert Hale, London, 1973 (o.p.)

Sutton, Graham, *Shepherd's Warning*, Collins, London, 1946 (o.p.); *Smoke Across the Fell*, Collins, 1947 (o.p.); *North Star*, Collins, 1949 (o.p.); *Fleming of Honister*, Hodder & Stoughton, London, 1953 (o.p.); *The Rowan Tree*, Hodder & Stoughton, 1958 (o.p.).

Trescatheric, Bryn, *Walney: A Wall in the Sea*, Hougenai Press, Barrow, 1984

West, Thomas, *The Antiquities of Furness*, The Author, Dalton, 1774 (o.p.); *Guide to the Lakes*, Law, London, 1784 (o.p.)

Westfields Nature Trails Guide, Barrow Council, undated (o.p.)

Wood, Oliver, *West Cumberland Coal*, CWAAS Extra Series XXIV, Cumberland & Westmorland Antiquarian & Archaeological Society, Kendal, 1988

Wordsworth, William, *The Poems* (2 volumes), Penguin, Harmondsworth, 1977; *Guide to the Lakes*, OUP, 1835 (Paperback edition, 1977)

Wyatt, John, *The Lake District National Park*, Webb & Bower/Michael Joseph, Exeter, 1987

INDEX